THE *Language* OF *Tides*

NEW & SELECTED POEMS

Lois Parker Edstrom

MoonPath Press

Poetry
ISBN 978-1-936657-64-3

Cover photo: "Point No Point Sunset" by Ronda Broatch
http://Ronda-Broatch.pixels.com

Author photo: Mel Edstrom

Book design: Tonya Namura using Leander Script Pro and Avenir (display) and Garamond Premier Pro (text)

MoonPath Press is dedicated to publishing the finest poets living in the U.S. Pacific Northwest.

MoonPath Press
PO Box 445
Tillamook, OR 97141

MoonPathPress@gmail.com

http://MoonPathPress.com

THE Language OF Tides

For my family

With gratitude for your love and
boundless ways of fostering laughter.

CONTENTS

New Poems

WITNESS TO MYSTERY	5
THE LANGUAGE OF TIDES	6
THE QUESTION OF BROKENESS	8
ORDINARY MORNING	9
SIMPLE PLEASURES	10
SUMMER FOG	11
LILACS	12
BRIGHT SECRET	13
SMALL TOWN BUSINESS	14
LENIENT GARDENER	15
ONE PERSON PARTY	17
ALMOST UNLIMITED VISION	19
HONEST WORK	20
LETTING GO	21
NEOWISE COMET	22
WHEN ALL HAS BEEN SAID	23
THE BELLS OF SUMMER	24
THE TURN OF SEASONS	25
ONLY ONCE	26
NOT WITHOUT A STRUGGLE	27
THROUGH THE TRAIN WINDOW	28
CARRYING AN AVALANCHE	29
AFTER THE STORM	30
SYMBOLS OF THINGS REMEMBERED	31

MOUNTAIN AIR   33

UNEARTHING HISTORY   34

OUT OF PLACE   35

PAUL GAUGUIN   36

FATA MORGANA   38

A PUZZLE   39

SILLY GRANDMA   40

MARRIAGE VOW   41

NEW LIFE   42

CHOOSE ME   43

From
WHAT BRINGS US TO WATER, 2010

WHEN ASKED WHY I WRITE POETRY   47

ADDIE MAY PARKER   48

FARM DOG   49

HOUSE OF GUESSES   50

WHAT BRINGS US TO WATER   51

DARK LULLABY   52

COOKIE BAKERS   53

OLD CHURCH PEW   54

MEMBER IN GOOD STANDING OF
THE SISTERHOOD   55

BEYOND ARTURO TOSCANINI'S BATON   56

SMITING DRAGONS   57

SUMMER MORNING ON THE FARM   58

From
WHAT'S TO BE DONE WITH BEAUTY, 2012

AMERICAN GOTHIC   61

PRIVATE MAN   63

POPPIES IN THE FOG   64

GREEN APPLE ON BLACK PLATE   66

STILL LIFE   67

HOLLYHOCKS   69

THE SECRET GARDEN   70

GARDEN SCENE   71

A SUNDAY ON LA GRANDE JATTE   72

INDIANS IN THE FOG   73

MONET'S GARDEN AT VETHEUIL   74

From
NIGHT BEYOND BLACK, 2016

CAFÉ TERRACE AT NIGHT   77

DAYBREAK   78

EROTICA IN UPTOWN   79

LUNCHEON ON THE GRASS   81

YESTERDAY'S LIGHT   82

SHE TURNED FIFTY   84

TILT   85

GARDEN PRANKS   87

WHERE POEMS WINTER   88

TAMARACK   89

EAST OF THE MOUNTAINS   90

CASCADE SUITE   91

WITHOUT NOTICE   92

BREATHE   93

BIOPSY   95

WHAT WE REMEMBER   96

THIS MOMENT OF GRACE   98

WINTER STILLNESS   99

ALMANAC   100

WHEN SILENCE WAS ENOUGH   101

GREEN '58 CHEVY APACHE TRUCK   102

CURRICULUM VITAE   103

HOMAGE TO PLATT ROGERS SPENCER   105

DOING DISHES   107

CHOICES WE MAKE WHEN WE ARE
TOO YOUNG TO MAKE THEM   108

TESTIMONY OF RAIN   110

SUBMERGED   111

From
GLINT, 2019

THE THEORY OF EVERYTHING   115

FLIGHT PATH   116

MIRABILIA   117

RIPE SEASON   118

NOVEMBER   119

FOG   120

WOLF MOON   121

A SMALL POEM ABOUT SOMETHING BIG   122

ALL OF IT   123

THE QUIET ONE   124

SMALL TOWN COFFEE HOUSE   125

IMPROVISATION   126

STRANGE BEDFELLOWS   127

PRAYER   128

ST. MARY'S AUTUMN RUMMAGE SALE   129

CONFESSIONS OF A YEASAYER   130

SMALL TOWN SATURDAY NIGHT   131

SEPTEMBER   132

THE FAR EDGE OF LONGING   133

NEBULOSITY   134

From
ROAD SIGNS AND HOBO MARKS, 2020

SONG FOR THE ROAD   137

THE GREAT DEPRESSION   138

HOBO PRIDE   139

MEANING OF A NAME   140

SHELTER   141

EXTENDED FAMILY   143

ON THE EDGE   144

BURLAP   145

THE BONE POLISHER   146

HARD SCRABBLE LIFE   147

DEAR BO   148

THE CAREGIVER   149

ROAD SIGNS AND HOBO MARKS   150

CHIMACUM 152

WHAT SOME CALL WILD 154

WELLINGTON ON STEVENS PASS 155

NOTES FROM A RAIN FOREST 157

WOODWORKER SPEAKS OF MARRIAGE 158

YELLOWSTONE PARK, 1948 159

COUNTERBALANCE 160

MOUNTAIN MAN IN TIE AND
WHITE JACKET 161

SOURDOUGH 162

DRIFT 163

From
THE LESSON OF PLUMS, 2020

FRAGILE WINGS 167

DEEP 169

THE QUIET CORE OF CHAOS 170

THE LESSON OF PLUMS 171

RED GIANTS AND WHITE DWARFS 172

AND THEY DANCED BY THE
LIGHT OF THE MOON 173

EBEY'S LANDING 174

IMPLICATIONS OF GLASS 175

THE WEIGHT OF WORDS 176

WHEN A MIRACLE SPEAKS 177

CONFESSION 178

DAMP MAGIC 180

GEOMETRY OF FAITH 181

THE WORLD BETWEEN   182

SYLLABLES OF WONDER   183

KINTSUGI   184

A GLORIOUS WEBBING   185

OPTICAL ILLUSION   187

THE QUESTION OF HAPPINESS   188

SPRING SOLSTICE   189

SHELTERING IN PLACE   190

DRAGONFLY   191

SETTING THINGS RIGHT   192

CIRCLE OF TWO   193

PARABLE OF A CARB LOVER   194

MIDDLE OF THE NIGHT MUSINGS   195

GENDER BIAS   197

EBEY'S PRAIRIE   198

THE ELEGANCE OF AGEING   199

WHY HAVE FAVORITES?   200

THE LONESOME TIME   201

THE SCENT OF MEMORIES   202

From
ALMANAC OF QUIET DAYS, 2021

NATURE'S HUSH   205

RIPENING SEASON   206

ROAD TRIP   207

AN INVITATION   208

HARVEST BEE   209

CATHEDRAL OF LIGHT   210

THE ENCHANTED FOREST   211

FENCES   212

BOOKWORM   213

FRAGILE BEAUTY   214

TREE HOUSE   215

MOUNT SHUKSAN   216

SNOW GEESE   217

COUNSEL TO A TEENAGER   218

A CURIOUS KNOWING   219

INNOVATION   220

PITCHFORK GRACE   221

POETS AND RODENTS   222

ONE ROOM   223

PEACEFUL VALLEY   224

Coda

AMETHYST   227

ACKNOWLEDGMENTS   229

ABOUT THE AUTHOR   233

THE Language OF Tides

New Poems

The task is to get through to the other side,
where we can hear the deep rhythms that
connect us with the stars and tides.

Stanley Kunitz

WITNESS TO MYSTERY

When I write I feel close to a mystery,
a vast, wide-winged unknown that hovers
just beyond my reach.

I don't need to understand. It is enough
to sense the clues scattered everywhere—
traces of a connected design that glitter,

an intimate secret waiting to be shared.
Often, it's small overlooked things:
beach grass and purple asters on the bluff,

a drop of dew clinging to the edge
of a Nootka rose. This morning I walk into fog
that wisps over the hill, charmed by foghorns,

a sonorous chorus of bass notes sounding across
Admiralty Inlet. Deep teal water swirls over rocks
at the edge of the shore. Now sunlight prances

across the rippling water and, not far out,
a pod of Orcas, sleek black and white bodies
breaching, plumes of spray like marine geysers

bursting skyward, images that follow me
to my writing room where time eases
away. On my desk a stack of white paper

and my black ink pen, elegant companions
that invite questions, and the wondrous
mystery lingers.

THE LANGUAGE OF TIDES

Tides, those ancient rhythms
that harmonize with the moon,
pull us toward an almost certain
reliability, yet a rogue wave
may overtake, the way sudden
trauma strikes without warning.

How unaware we are of silent menace,
and maybe that is as it should be—
that fear is not a presence pressing
against the bloom of joy.

Tides, such a glossary of surprises.
This morning, as I explore
the waves' donations,
I come upon a large concrete block
unmoored from a distant dock, tossed
upon the shore, a show of strength
from a restless sea.

And once, a beached whale, that mammoth
creature helpless and without options,
waited for the tide to rise to return
to the deep passage of the inlet.

Tides dictate the treacherous waters
of Deception Pass—a slack tide advised
to pass through and, like difficult choices,
it may be prudent to wait.

We become lulled by the sea's cradle song,
as tide charts clock the rise and fall
of the sea, a soothing rhythm we learn to trust,

yet we know the tide gives and takes:
its exclamations forceful,
its utterances bearing consequences.

THE QUESTION OF BROKENESS

Some call them flags, these irises
that unfurl their banners from sturdy
green staffs: purple, peach, white
and yellow as if each represents
a kingdom of beauty.

They rise from knobby beginnings
faithful and resilient, yet left
to their own devices, in their eagerness
to grow, the roots become tangled
and crowded into a tight, limiting mass.
They must be broken apart, planted
separately, given a new start.

How hard it is to disturb what seems
to be thriving, yet we never know
what lies below the surface until
we dig a little deeper—how kind faces,
shy smiles may cover a tangle
of hurt, bound by despair.

Some think we are all broken,
but I'm not sure that is true.
Perhaps we are frail and imperfect
and vulnerable to brokenness,

but we can rise from shattered expectations,
open to a place of deeper understanding
and the freedom to launch new beginnings.

ORDINARY MORNING

You could say it's an ordinary morning,
except it isn't. The sky opens like a hymnal
and summer sun streams into our tiny town,
blessing the cove and burnishing the shops
that perch on the bluff.

This sleepy town awakens to the light,
stretches its arms, ready to welcome
early risers. A shopkeeper adjusts
the sign on the bookstore. Folks
find an outdoor table at the coffee shop,
greet friends that gather there each morning.
I stop at the bakery: molasses oat bread,
warm and fragrant, placed into my hands.

Years ago, tall ships sailed into our cove,
exchanging goods and stories of distant places.
Historic homes still line the hillside.
You can almost hear the voices of early settlers
and sea captains falling in love with the island.

Nearing home, fog spreads a froth
of white lace in the inlet and skims
my skin with freshness. From a neighbor's
roadside stand, I raise a lavish bouquet
of sweet peas to my face, breathe in
all the sweetness of this not quite
ordinary morning.

SIMPLE PLEASURES

A sailboat glides into Penn Cove,
its white sail a crisp contrast against
the deep blue water and beyond,
the snowy cone of Mount Baker.

From where I sit on the bluff, I hear
the distant thud of a hammer striking
wood. Someone is mending or building,
when elsewhere much is being taken apart.

I catch the scent of fish frying.
Someone is attending to basic needs
and perhaps the satisfaction
of good food, well-prepared.

During this time of quarantine, I reflect
on how simple pleasures take on more
significance. At the dinner table my son
hums as he eats, his unique expressions
of praise add gold stars to my recipes
and illuminate my book of satisfaction.

Now the sailboat tacks out of the cove
plying the calm waters of this summer day,
its destination unknown to me, and there is
no need to know. From the beginning
we swim in strange, uncharted waters,
yet somehow, we find our way.

SUMMER FOG

Fog has enclosed the island for days,
not soft white tatters that drift
and float, filled with refreshing
moisture, but fog that hangs
in thick brown curtains and carries
the acrid scent of flaming forests
torched by wild fires devouring
parts of the mainland.

This morning the lake is visible,
and beyond, sunlight glints off the bay
spilling through clouds that part
and shift in ever changing shapes.

For a time, the isolation felt eerily cozy,
then became oppressive
like the relentless presence of wind,
an intrusion that calls attention to itself
and becomes fatiguing.

LILACS

As I walked down Main Street of our small town,
an old-fashioned lilac brushed my shoulder
and carried me on a carpet of fragrance
back to my sixth-grade classroom.

A vase of lilacs graced Miss Reece's desk,
lilacs the exact color of her trim suit.
A froth of white lace bloomed at her neck,
secured by a floral brooch. The lace resembled
her chalk-white hair.

We read poetry in Miss Reece's class.
We memorized poems, wrapped in the fragrance
of lilacs. I didn't realize it then, that Miss Reece
and her love of kids and poetry, would reach deep
into my life, not perceptible until much later.

It took me a long time to find out what had been there
all along—a love of poetry that goes beyond
the reading—words that come from somewhere else,
show up on the page and are somehow mine.

Like the brooch that fastened the lace around
Miss Reece's neck, poetry pinned me to bliss.

BRIGHT SECRET

I don't know him, this young man
with the curly hair, but when I see him
in town from time to time,
he is always smiling.

This evening he is at the beach. He is alone.
He stands in profile backlit by the sun.
A servant of summer, his face glows,
as if he entertains a bright secret
he is about to serve up on a platter
of good fortune and gratitude.

Now in sunlit rays skittering across the bay,
in that perfect moment when all is aligned,
he opens his mouth, the light enters,
and he swallows the sun.

SMALL TOWN BUSINESS

On my early morning walk, I didn't see
the baker proofing yeast.

I didn't see the pizza guy stretching
dough or the florist arranging flowers.

Through the bookstore window, I didn't see
the shopkeeper reading or, at the post office,

the mailman sorting mail. I didn't see the jailer
checking locks or the brew master sampling beer.

The banker was not counting money,
nor was the inn keeper making beds.

All was quiet near the market, and on the wharf
the harbor master was nowhere to be seen.

I did see the barber warming up, getting ready
for his day, a large electric hedge clipper in hand,

expertly and precisely trimming the hedge
in front of his shop.

LENIENT GARDENER

The vegetables in my garden line up
in straight rows like obedient
school children assembling for recess.

Beans crawl up poles, wrapping
themselves tightly into place.

Peas send out tendrils that reach
toward twine, tendrils that twist
and turn, creating a durable bond.

Tomatoes rely on the support of stakes,
producing a glow of vermillion globes
within wire cages.

I shelter the vegetables behind a fenced plot,
safe from deer and rabbits.

Vegetables must behave, but certain flowers
are like free-range kids—they roam.

Cerinthe, a wild child with glorious
purple-blue blossoms fading to lavender,
causes me to overlook its faults.
It grows, abundantly and unexpectedly,
where it shouldn't.

I never know where the purple poppies
will appear; seeds scattered years ago
by two designing five-year-olds.

These gorgeous poppies grow unhampered
in every flower bed and between the cracks
of stepping stones. They have a flamboyant

smugness, as if they are saying, *I'll grow
anywhere I want. I'll keep you guessing.*

My friend and neighbor has a well-tended
garden—everything in its intended place.
Roses diligently pruned, each a sculptural
masterpiece, honeysuckle clings to the arbor,
lupines stay in their own little patch of land.
All is carefully planned and beautiful.

I am a lenient gardener.
Even as bearded iris, narcissus,
and catmint overflow their space,
and rosemary grows to shrub size,
muscling in on other herbs, I prize
my garden. Like everyday life, I want
to be surprised by the unexpected,
able to enjoy what doesn't quite fit,
and welcome the displaced.

ONE PERSON PARTY

The day breaks bright and clear,
an August morning that whispers
with selfish possibilities.

I splurge, pouring cream
on my oatmeal rather than
one percent.

Dark roast coffee with Meyers lemon
biscotti at my desk, I settle in
to write.

Time passes without notice, words
intoxicating me, taking me
on unexpected journeys far
from my writing room.

Later, I ease into the cast iron tub,
steamy and fragrant with lavender soap.
From the window over the tub
I see the neighbor's windmill
and the rose thicket by the barn.

I wander out to the porch, settle
onto the chaise lounge, and tuck
into the pages of a novel. I nap.

I read more. Nap again,
and it isn't even noon.
This afternoon I plan to devour
a Cherries Jubilee hot fudge sundae.

Yes, it's my birthday. I've received
cards, gifts, and expressions

of love, but I also choose to honor
myself doing many of the things
I like best—such selfish,
once a year, possibilities.

ALMOST UNLIMITED VISION

From the window above my writing table
Mount Rainier is a massive presence
that only appears when clouds move away
to reveal its dominating form. How can
something so immovable come as a surprise?

Further north, beyond the waters that surround
this island, the peaks of Whitehorse, Three Fingers,
and Mount Pilchuck are familiar snow-capped
beacons from my childhood.

Some years ago, when summer had removed
its cloak of snow, I climbed Mount Pilchuck
with a friend. Above the tree line, the slope
was spangled with wild blueberries and we ate,
our mouths like clown-mouths painted purple.

As we climbed, a green valley spread out below:
a river, a farmhouse, and the quiet freedom of isolation.
We reached the summit, climbed a ladder that led
to the platform of a fire-watch tower perched
on a craggy prominence.

I followed my friend, but found I could not move
to the final rung of the ladder. *Come up,* she said.
*You need to add your name to the others
who have been here.*

The lookout, balanced as it seemed in air,
felt too risky. I couldn't find the courage
to take the final step.

HONEST WORK

There was a time I thought I had no regrets.
If I left, I'd be traveling lightly.
I was young.

Time has a way of backlighting memories. Tiny
acts, not intentionally hurtful, but thoughtless.
I was young.

Words scattered like chicken feed at the feet
of those I may have hurt by indiscretion.
I was young.

Frustration that showed its unkind face, spewed
remarks that should have been left unsaid.
I was young.

Regret is like moss. It grows and flourishes
in dark places. Forgiveness is honest work
yielding a deep harvest,

however, it's sometimes difficult
to offer grace to yourself.

LETTING GO

The wind, a persistent blow,
slows my footsteps.

I lean into the resistance,
no angry gusts, rather

a steady pressure that alters
the evergreens into stark

sculptures of rigidity.
As I turn around, head

in another direction,
the resistance becomes grace,

pushing me along like a teacher's
rewarding pat on the back

as if I'd figured it out,
found the right answer.

NEOWISE COMET

July 17, 2020

In the northwest sky
under the Big Dipper

the brilliance, the gases,
the light.

Such energy and movement
ablaze in the blackness of night.

Some things seem too spectacular
to approach with words.

Stanley Kunitz, my poetic hero,
when waiting for Halley's Comet

as a child, was told by his teacher,
if it wandered off its course

and smashed into the earth
there'd be no school tomorrow.

I had never seen a comet, and I suspect
I will never see another.

Neowise left a question mark slashed
across the sky. I think about how

wonderment can disguise peril and how,
unsuspectingly, we may brush up against danger

without ever recognizing our vulnerability.

WHEN ALL HAS BEEN SAID

Mariposa Monarca, Monarch Butterfly
~Paulette Turco

What else can we say about the butterfly?
So familiar, the intricate

black and orange design, fragile wings
rimmed with white dots,

the butterfly's well-known symbolism,
and metaphor of transformation.

Yet, when a butterfly alights nearby
it is like an unexpected visit

from a sovereign head of state,
a monarch in our midst.

Like a strange angel,
it suddenly appears

carrying a message of vulnerability
and beauty.

Its essence enters the body, a fluttering
that accelerates the heart.

THE BELLS OF SUMMER

Stand under the pear tree. Look up
through its tracery of branches. The sky
winks in triangles of light, and pears
hang like bells chiming summer's
green sweetness.

Dare to cut the dense skin, feel the syrupy
white flesh as it glides over your tongue
and the juice that trickles down your chin.

Forget about napkins and stains on your shirt.
Gather the bliss of summer's bounty into
your mouth, swallow what's left before

autumn comes, shakes out its apron
of flamboyant leaves, trying to trick you
into thinking it has something better to offer.

THE TURN OF SEASONS

Summer is trailing the tatters
of what had been thriving; now fields
dried to the color of tobacco, dust
and smoke sifting through the still air.

The garden climbs over itself
in a rush to be finished, squash vines
scaling the fence and infiltrating
the honeysuckle. Zinnias, cosmos,
and bachelor buttons competing
for dominance.

The lines are slacking off at the ice cream
shop, and the bookstore's open doors
will soon be closed to the salty gusts
that blow in from the cove.

It is difficult to put away the outdoor games
and kites, remembering the children
romping in our fields, and the sheer joy
of their laughter.

Soon it will be time to gather around the hearth
as the ancients have done for centuries,
settle into a cave of well-being, warmed
by fires of gratitude.

ONLY ONCE

Autumn does not brag about itself
on Whidbey Island. No flashy splashes
of color in the forests, mostly the quiet
calm of evergreens.

At the shore waves curl upon themselves,
an ancient rhythm that echoes within
the chambers of the heart, and the salty
breath of the sea needs no freshener.

Now, the memory of a small boy,
a brief open-faced expression
that made me feel I was beautiful
beyond words.

These fleeting moments: the crackle
of hearth fire, the fragrance of the freshly
mown field, the gladness in my husband's
eyes when we meet at day's end,
the uninhibited laughter of a child.

This morning I wander through the forest
near our home, notice an alder leaf
detach from the tree.

The leaf slowly descends, swaying
in a mild breeze, a pirouette, a delicate
ballet performed on a cool autumn day,
and the thing is, this particular leaf
only does that once.

NOT WITHOUT A STRUGGLE

The Wenatchee River pours through Tumwater Canyon,
a persistent downward passage to the Columbia.
Autumn has splashed the canyon with golden light,
setting the maples ablaze.

On a bridge that crosses the river we look down
through clear water; silent torpedo-shaped
salmon sway against the current,
the yearly ritual of spawning.

They seek quiet pools upstream, in the curls
of the river's drama, a shaded place
to lay their eggs, then die, bodies
battered by the struggle.

This season of letting go, of release, is never
easy, maples flaunting brave banners before
dropping to the ground, and what of us?
Some say letting go is a part of love,

and this may be true—a quiet acceptance
that grants the gift of freedom to grown children
and past regrets, yet often we hold tightly
to what we love, and letting go becomes
a heartbreaking sacrifice of necessity.

THROUGH THE TRAIN WINDOW

Through the train window the world clicks by
in fast-moving snapshots. Black and white Holsteins
dot farmlands like orcas in a sea of pasture.

In the foothills, shanties cluster close to the tracks,
tilted toward the clack and clatter of wheels
on rails, a familiar rhythm of possibilities
and distant destinations.

The rivers rage, threatening to overflow
their banks as we ascend into the mountains—
jagged pinnacles piercing clouds and sky.
This November evening, darkness comes early
and deepens as we enter the Cascade Tunnel,
eight miles of dense blackness beneath
the snow-packed peaks.

When we emerge, Christmas lights glimmer
in the distance and the train slows down
to allow travelers to disembark in a small village
on the other side of the summit.

How quickly life streams by. We understand
only a small part of what's around us, as we cling
to beauty, endure dark spaces, and continue on,
so grateful for light.

CARRYING AN AVALANCHE

Why am I crying? For a time, the mind
escapes the reality of loss, but the heart

holds on, unable to unburden itself,
pain lodged deep in the recesses

of sadness like a mountain
holding back an avalanche of snow.

I wonder how long,
knowing there is no answer.

It's like calling for help only to hear
the echo of your own voice.

Outside, the bay is the color of often-washed
denim fading to gray and the island,

which rarely feels the flutter of snowflakes,
is shrouded in deep snow and isolating coldness,

which began on Christmas Day, continued
until New Year's Eve, when savage winds

raged throughout the night, a fury
that gave no sign of relenting.

I awake to silence. The wind has cleared
the fields of snow and the roads are passable.

AFTER THE STORM

After a night of scant sleep, much pain,
you submit to the prods and probes
of various doctors, the explorations
of tech-age machines, the ministrations
of nurses, the hopeful relief of medications.

Home once again, after three days on the edge
of a knife, you ask to go to Ebey's Landing,
where, during the night a storm heaped driftwood
far up on the shore, braided kelp into glistening
serpent-like mounds.

After hours of punishing wind and a wild deluge
of rain, the surf is tame, a gentle ruffling
like the flounce of a lacy petticoat, and the waves
are but a whisper.

How simply the sea calms itself once the storm
has passed, and in the morning light gumweed shines
through beach grass like gold stars.

SYMBOLS OF THINGS REMEMBERED

A small wooden pepper grinder graces
our table. Some say, *things don't matter.*
We collect too much.

I have learned certain things do matter.
Regrets linger for items I no longer have:
a tattered green monkey, a childhood comfort
I callously threw away when I was a young
adult and less sentimental.

I wish I had kept my mother's tap shoes
after she died, a way to touch the joyous
part of her life that dancing nurtured.

My sons' childhood books were given
to a needy family, yet I wish I had kept
a few of the favorites as a way to recapture
the essence of those precious story times.

Even my wedding dress was dispatched
as I cleaned and organized and decided
what was dispensable, thinking space
was more important than sentiment.

The wooden pepper grinder has become
a quiet symbol of remembrance.
Given to me by my beloved grandmother,
it traced back to her neighbor and friend,
Mrs. Wallace.

Mrs. Wallace was a Gold Star Mother, her son,
Joe, killed during the Second World War.
Who knows what was said or the strength
of the bond between these two women
as they grieved the loss of Joe.

Our government booked passage
for Gold Star Mothers to visit the graves
of sons buried in France. Mrs. Wallace
left her secluded farm to make the voyage.

The small wooden pepper grinder crossed
the ocean, coming back from France to the U.S.
with the grieving mother who placed it
into my grandmother's hands.
I understand now why some *things* do matter.

MOUNTAIN AIR

Lake Crescent serpentines for eleven miles
around the base of evergreen-clad mountains
on the peninsula of Washington State.

After the war, Vietnam vets hid out
in these remote, dense forests. I wonder
if they are still here. I can't begin to imagine
the depth of their anguish, or how it would feel
to be always on high alert.

A duck waddles over to where my sweetheart
and I are enjoying a picnic on the shore
of the lake. It is as if she knew we had fresh
almond croissants and oat bread in our lunch basket.

She walks with a toe-in swag, as if she knows
how to get what she wants. We throw her bits
of bread, then notice a sign: *Don't feed
the wild life.*

As I sit by the edge of the water, I can feel
the quiet that curls like morning mist
in the mountain air. May it follow the wounded
men, who learned to survive in these forests,
and bless them with rest.

UNEARTHING HISTORY

In the night, I imagine the musical tinkle
of harnesses and the nicker of horses
as they are led to the cart. I can almost feel
the damp clouds of their breath and the slick
satin shine of their haunches.

The stables of Fort Casey occupied our land
in 1914. A gate, hidden in the rose thicket
at the corner of our acreage, must have allowed
the passage of many horses.

Our friend Bill explores our land
with a metal detector. He finds horseshoes,
decorative pieces from carts and carriages,
a brass harness rosette stamped US Army,
now housed in a glass case at the museum.

I like to think of horses grazing in our fields
and the bits of history buried below the surface.
As I dig in my garden, soil sifting through
my fingers, I find no military artifacts, but I feel
a rush of pleasure as I unearth russets and red
potatoes, lifting them from their trenches,
such ordinary edible treasures.

OUT OF PLACE

Dawn has taken leave of darkness,
given up its gentleness to ruptured
sunlight, and in the western sky

the full moon is as bright as the sun.
Odd how lunar dependability
can seem altered when viewed

in an uncommon setting.
Like a flamboyant jokester in a tranquil
space, the moon seems out of place,

as if resisting the cycle of change.
Exposed, in a golden sky, it has lost
the shine of silver rays dancing

across the lake at midnight. Yet the moon,
steady as a drumbeat, continues its rhythms,
and we are bound by the pull

of its rotations as surely as the tides that lap
the shores of our island. Oh, perception,
my flawed, unreliable companion.

PAUL GAUGUIN

Some try to separate the man,
the myth, the art
as if one could separate
a sorcerer from his magic.

Isn't there always more
than one truth?
What I am to you
may not be what I am
to someone else.

Gauguin's certainty reverberates
in Polynesia like a bell once struck
that chimes in circles rippling outward.

He visits cerebral rooms of quiet
Polynesian women who belong
as sisters of *The Big Tree*, keepers
of a bridgeless span to *Sacred Springs,*
The Sacred Mountain.

Who can deny *Whispered Words*
that move into strokes of passion,
a texture we see, but only in part.

Reclining Tahitian Women
infuse the paintings with rest;
a languorous ebb of bathers,
white horses, *Still Life*
with Exotic Birds.

He paints *The Moment of Truth*
and what was that for him?
How can we hope to dip
our brushes into the color of his
life, gain access to the paint pots
of another?

FATA MORGANA

We don't know what to make of Morgan le Fay
who is able to change shape and fly.
Like all of us, she is an amalgam
of questionable behaviors, although most of us
don't rise to the villainous state.

The sister of King Arthur, the apprentice
of Merlin, she floats through the centuries
casting magical powers over clouds,
and oceans, skewing the wits of seafarers.

I consider how weather currents shift
one over the other to create castles
in the sky, like day dreams that float
just under the surface of our consciousness.

To this day, Morgan le Fay schemes
her way into the atmosphere, forming images
on the horizon: cities, mountain ranges,
and sailing ships that drift upside down.

She is a healer, an enchantress, a sorceress,
a powerful schemer. In quiet interior battles,
let's hope goodness rises to ascendancy.

A PUZZLE

I have never liked crossword puzzles.
How can that be? my friends and family ask
of a woman who is dazzled by words.

It is curious, I admit, but I like to coax
words into interesting relationships
rather than look for missing parts.

My son cajoled me into joining him
in his early morning practice of working
a puzzle from the newspaper. Big sigh,
and I began the mother-son bonding
process of across and down.

He finished his puzzle well ahead of me.
I was stuck in the upper left-hand corner
of mine. I persevered, and with him looking
over my shoulder, he watched as I contemplated
the letters *n-e-p-t* of the last word I needed
to complete the puzzle. With a flourish,
amid his uproarious laughter, I added the *i*.

SILLY GRANDMA

We vowed we wouldn't do it—
gush about the extraordinary charm
and achievements of our grandchildren.

It turns out we are among the worst.
I won't tell you how, when our grandson
was six, he asked to take the sack of treats
Santa had given him to the library
to give to the poor kids.

I won't tell you how, as a teenager,
he worked alongside his grandpa
framing, wiring, and shingling our house.

I won't tell you how he chose difficult
math and science classes at the university,
then followed a path as a successful
software engineer.

I won't even mention that he met and married
a lovely young woman who shares his values,
and together they are building a fine home
as they look forward to the arrival of children.

Just allow me a memory that has stayed with me
all these years: When he was a year old,
separated by distance, and unable
to be together for some time, I wondered
if he would recognize me.

When I picked him up he put his cheek against mine—
remembering how we had danced.

MARRIAGE VOW

Something was written
in the afterlife of promise

not immediately apparent
until years later

a gradual realization
something deeper

something finer
solid unshakeable

weighted by certainty
proven by a deed of trust

inscribed with the ink
of kindness and forgiveness.

It was hidden amidst
the fragrance of roses

the shine of satin
the gleam of candles

eagerness to fashion
a new life together

and now the years have exposed
that afterlife of promise

stamped indelibly
in the ledger of our lives

resilient beyond imagining.

NEW LIFE

Spring opens the season's door to effervescence.
In the woods, deciduous trees, long silent

under the cloak of winter, break into clouds
of green froth, and dandelions seem intent

on conquering the fields with battalions
of spangled suns.

Peonies rise from their long sleep
as if awakened by a prince's kiss.

Even the old curmudgeons who sit
on the bench by the post office

sniff the air as if they are on the trail
of something acceptable,

and children run in the school yard,
their laughter an assurance that all is well

and all will be well. The season rushes
toward us so full of promise

it is almost more than one can bear,
and I think of Brother David Steindl-Rast,

the Benedictine monk, who said:
We do not die from death, but from fully ripened love.

CHOOSE ME

I don't know if I find them
or they find me. Poems are everywhere,
just waiting to be noticed.

Relentless in their persistence,
their beautiful voices plead,
Choose me, Choose me.

They interrupt my sleep, my bath time,
appointments, time with friends. It seems
they are intimate companions.

Open to discussion and compromise,
they are adamantly protective of the truth.
If I hesitate, they disappear, hidden
in the folds of memory.

I want to honor them, give them the time
and space they deserve, these worthy
messengers of art and awe-struck
admirers of nature.

Sometimes they sing, and that I cannot
ignore: lyrics that float through the air,
rhythms that beat in sync with my heart.

From

WHAT BRINGS US TO WATER
2010

WHEN ASKED WHY I WRITE POETRY

After Lisel Mueller

I say, because the sea urchin, cracked
and forgotten, reveals glistening
cathedral arches;

because crows sorrowing
on the fence for a brother
felled by a farmer's shot
teach the meaning of black,

and from waves, I learn
of rattle and release;

because the dragonfly that rests
with its wings open compels me
to speak of vulnerability,

and the marjoram in my garden
beads itself into spicy splendor;

because my hands
take on utilitarian beauty
wringing out a washcloth;

because each step is praise
to movement;

because the one-pound fawn
cut from its dead mother's stomach
breathes,

and the scent of a single violet
crushed underfoot is drenched
salvation.

ADDIE MAY PARKER

1867–1896, Oso, Washington

Whitehorse Mountain hollows out the sky,
spreads a deep shadow upon the farmlands
of the Stillaguamish Valley, as does the death
of my great-grandmother.

The river took her, an undertow of questions
only Mrs. Bennett, the neighbor, could answer.
*The canoe overturned as we were crossing
the river*, she said.

History scribbles a hasty note: estimable lady,
devoted husband, three small sons—
my grandfather and his twin brothers.
Death: accidental.

Her taffeta wedding gown hangs in my armoire,
whispers *touch me, touch me,* as if fingertips
could link the past, this child-sized dress—
strong fabric, meticulous stitches, covered buttons.

My grandfather never spoke of the accident,
the story stacked between generations,
until I asked. *She was deathly afraid of the river,*
he said. *Would never voluntarily*

have stepped into a canoe.

FARM DOG

That old collie never learned—
some things are too electrifying
to be pursued.

Once again, loping down the hill,
out of the woods, muzzle barbed
with quills.

He just couldn't stop
nipping at that exotic
creature.

I think of Tip,
how he knew more pain
to come in the shape of pliers.

I understand that dog
nipping at joy. It's worth
the wounds.

HOUSE OF GUESSES

The framework gone, the house
lingers like the scent of rain on dry earth.
A golden pool of daffodils laps
at the edge of phantom rooms;
old lilacs trace where walls once stood.

I'm drawn to this field above the cove
where time has removed joists and rafters,
the foundation oriented to the land
the way long married couples always choose
a fixed side of the bed, amending
themselves to each other.

Wild cherry trees lean
toward the clearing as if listening
to voices from the past,
those who scrubbed the doorstep
with bristled sorrow, loved
as they knew how,
and belonged to this soil
where they have buried
their stories.

WHAT BRINGS US TO WATER

There is a capillary tug
to be at water's edge
this low tide day, sand sculpted
into waves impersonating
those that retreat.
What do I hope to find
as the watery skin of earth
is pulled back by the moon,
exposing bone and sinew of the sea?
Calcified knobs, plates, and shafts
are strewn along the shore, fractured
detritus of life that was.
A crab shell the color
of dried blood rests atop
seaweed pooled like bile,
and a breeze blows
a briny breath along
the rumpled shore.
Silver rivulets run seaward
to catch and be filled beyond
searching eyes and musings.
Glistening arteries join the pulse
and surge of tide, eclipsing
my footprints and my question.

DARK LULLABY

Fort George Wright Military Cemetery
Spokane, Washington

The babies peek at the world
and are gone.

No one knows what takes them.

In that decade, the fifties,
two hundred sixty-one babies
slipped away—the white stone
markers, mute testimony of their lives,
here on this hill that overlooks
the Spokane River and beyond.
The stillborn, so still,
and those who came early, their lungs
like butterfly wings fanning the air
a few hours,
a few days or weeks,
before folding,
calm on the current of a dark lullaby—
a bequeath of silence,
that space between the notes
of an unfamiliar melody,
and a memory
of pure love, undiluted by world.

COOKIE BAKERS

It's not the memory of the 1940s kitchen,
radio tuned to *Queen for a Day*,

or the *Betty Crocker Cookbook* splayed
beside the Sunbeam mixer.

Not even the fragrance of snickerdoodles,
hot from the oven, that summons

me, the child, yearning to lay my head,
one more time, on my mother's lap.

It's a husk of oatmeal that I find
between the pages of her cookbook

long after she's gone.

OLD CHURCH PEW

We stand for the benediction,
and throughout the sanctuary
fingers curve over the top rail,

young and old hands linked
on the fore pew like daisy-chains
in a field of stained glass light.

The grainy oak rail where
my hands rest is marred
by imperfections: a gouge

from a worker's tool, a blemish
that grew with the tree,
an embedded nail.

The rail has been rubbed smooth
by generations of seekers—
those who depend on it for support,

those gaining leverage to rise, others
who ease themselves down to rest,
some just holding on.

MEMBER IN GOOD STANDING OF
THE SISTERHOOD

I don't remember being this kind of girl.
Raising sons, I may have forgotten how it was.

My three-year-old granddaughter whispers secrets
in my ear, brushes my hair, slathers my legs with lotion,

chooses my earrings, sparkly tees, and says,
You shouldn't stay so long in the tub.

It causes wrinkles.

BEYOND ARTURO TOSCANINI'S BATON

She fancies herself a diva—
arms outstretched,
red satin gloves that rise
like the flames of *Die Walkure*.

Her voice ascends, glides up
to the highest range
and lingers there, the volume
belying her slight,
four-year-old body.
Then staccato punches,
the notes like tin stars heaved
against an aluminum moon.

She pauses, assesses her audience,
You'll know I'm done
when I do the splits.

Take that, La Scala.

SMITING DRAGONS

They fashion pope hats from the morning newspaper—
fold, staple, and tape until their headgear rises

like spires pointing toward heaven: Daddy's crimson
from a Target ad, Emily's a mosaic of cartoons.

Rolling the remaining papers into rubber-banded weapons,
they set off on their quest. They search under the piano,

behind the couch, beneath the beds, hoping
to roust the dragon from its hiding place.

They need only to point, and the force of their courage zings
out the end of their rods to zap

the silver-scaled dragon into submission
where it lies curled around the bright jewels of their day.

SUMMER MORNING ON THE FARM

Those distant years, I saw a charm
of goldfinch lift all at once from the lilac,
gold coins flung into the air
and felt bits of myself spin away.

I knelt in the shadow of the porch,
touched the velvet chambers
of a bleeding heart and sensed its pulse
as my own.

Honeysuckle claimed the woodshed,
clinging to spaces between the weathered
shingles, tendrils trailing from the roof.

The fragrance muscled through the open
window. Eight years old, asleep in a plain
iron bed, I smelled it before opening my eyes—
the bold extravagance. I've never recovered.

From

WHAT'S TO BE DONE WITH BEAUTY
2012

Ekphrastic Poems

AMERICAN GOTHIC

1930, Oil on Beaverboard
The Art Institute of Chicago
Grant Wood, 1891-1942

Grant Wood, look
what you've done to these people
constrained between pitchfork,
and there beyond that gothic window,
beyond those trees,
the shadow of a steeple.

The unmarried daughter standing
slightly behind her father,
cameo at junction of white collar,
hears worried whispers
from the past, but along the slender
neck, a wisp of hair escapes
your brush and her tending;
she can let it all down, desire
zig-zagging behind that shuttered gaze
like rick-rack on her apron.

And the father, the farmer
so solemn, tight-buttoned,
proper. He has lived
within the art, obedient
to your vision, his pockets filled
with mercy, and the work-hardened
hand remembers the tender
curve of his bride in night's light,
long ago, hungering behind
that lace curtain.

These two, the father
and the daughter, rise
from the oil, tint, and toil
of their existence, parting pigment,
tracing longings within rigid lines,
voices in undertone compelling
us to know—we are not
what we seem, we are
so much more.

PRIVATE MAN

The Dinner Horn
1870, Oil on Canvas
Winslow Homer, 1836-1910

That young girl standing in sunlight,
the dinner horn pressed to her lips,
a crescent of dark striped underskirt
revealed beneath her soft white dress.
Is she calling to workers in the field
or to the reclusive artist who preferred
painting *en plein air*?

He held the details of his life in a tight fist,
releasing parts of himself
only when he picked up a brush,
filled, as he was, with light and shadow,
lines connecting the complex parts
of himself.

How else those first paintings
to arrive fully formed?
Detail, like the perfection
of a fetal fingernail—the inner life
of his subjects emerging the way
nests appear when leaves forsake
the trees of winter.

POPPIES IN THE FOG

2012, Photograph by Mel Edstrom

Fog slips through the Strait of Juan de Fuca,
settles itself in Admiralty Inlet,

and eases over our part of the island,
a cocooning of fields and house

until hard edges soften
like the easing of long held pain

and everything quiets down—
a private world where

what lies ahead is obscured
and we are satisfied

with not knowing.
The foghorn's muffled

lament close, then more distant—
a curious comfort, and from the shore,

on the incoming tide, I see
a heron floating by on driftwood.

Now fog fills our gardens
where purple poppies cup

this fragile ration of sky
and silver dewdrops bead

the blooms, poise
on jade leaves, slide down

the stem of spent blossoms,
each pod a vault

of silent explosions.

GREEN APPLE ON BLACK PLATE

1921, Oil on Canvas
Birmingham Art Museum, Alabama
Georgia O'Keefe 1887-1986

You look upon this apple as a god—
reverential washing, one sacrificial slice
exposing moon-white halves,
four brown seeds cupped in translucent pods.
Then, careful paring and separation,
thin green-rimmed crescents fanned on black plate;
communion offered to those of us who wait.

I consider past transgressions:
the pleasure of a lusty bite,
the crunch and slurp of apple gouged
by teeth and ravished to the core,
to the stem and withered blossom end.

STILL LIFE

1942, Oil on Copper
Frida Kahlo, 1907-1954

So, the painting is controversial.
So, the president's wife sent it back,
the commissioned piece meant

for an honored place in the palace.
So, a friend acquired it.
Then it went missing.

This carefully arranged viscera,
the anatomy of ripeness,
of life, of small deaths.

Fruits and vegetables
that somehow become
more than they are.

Fingered fronds wave
like sea anemones against
the teal background, float

and open, fallopian ballerinas
poised to net a seed, now implanted
in the squash's moist cavity.

Soft folds of bloom, gonadic plums,
the lime's distended nipple,
pale lips, and the pear's puckered

blossom end. A Polyphemus moth
hovers above, seeks ripe flesh
to lay her eggs, then die.

After Frida's death
the painting was found,
hidden for years on the canopy

above her bed.

HOLLYHOCKS

1911, Oil on Canvas
National Academy of Design, New York
Fredrick Frieseke, 1874 - 1939

My one idea...is to produce the effect of vibration.

Hear the vibration of sunlight flickering
among hollyhocks, an indefinable pip

which plants itself in furrows of the brain
the way a seed, that casket of rebirth,

opens to amenable soil. The woman,
elegant as the garden, touches a flower—

a tuft of bells, a chiming swell,
striations of the heart

tremble, steal thunder
from the mouth.

What's to be done with beauty?

THE SECRET GARDEN

Illustrations by Tasha Tudor

Sorrow fills her, the way moss
fills the cracks of a long-forgotten
path. She pulls back the shelter
of ivy, the clutch of deep-rooted
grief, kneels in a secluded garden,
fingers stained with the rust of loss.
Here, green intention, cosseted
in a bulb's womb, makes its way
to light, blossoms in a barren space.

We are saved by many things:
a convent of silence, the grit
of experience, how a flute's
silver note penetrates the secret,
and a crow can bear witness
to our darkness.

GARDEN SCENE

2007, Abstract Watercolor on Paper
Private Collection
John Ringen, 1928–

You can almost hear chords
of color descend into the garden
from the thrum of hummingbird wings.

Delphinium's saturated blue beam,
cerinthe oozing violet blood,
monarda's inferno.

The bird dips and lifts
above purple flames
of penstemon and salvia.

You don't need to see it to know
crickets fiddle an old-world tune
against the tremolo of bees.

Rest, you want only to feel
the curious beat and rhythm
of growth.

Trust me,
a watering can waits
beside the garden chair.

A SUNDAY ON LA GRANDE JATTE

1884-86, Oil on Canvas
The Art Institute, Chicago
George Seurat, 1859-1891

Marbles cradled in the hand scatter
into a sheen of silence.

Only the spherical colors shout
as children play, the spangle
of their laughter swept
into quiet contemplation
by the tip of the artist's brush.
Such silence.

Bugle notes swallowed by a gentle
sky, and the rustle of fashionable bustles
rounded in soundless elegance.
Small whirls of color create a universe
that tricks the eye, hoodwinks
even the monkey, into harmonious
stillness.

INDIANS IN THE FOG

1965, Charcoal on Paper
Private Collection
Brian Edstrom, 1961–

Two smiling Indians paddle a canoe.
Nearby an alligator swims in stylized waves,

returns a friendly grin. A quick sweep of the artist's hand
across charcoaled paper has caused a sudden shift

in weather. Only a duck flying through clouds
seems dissatisfied with its progress.

Four years old, he's on to new adventures.
Swift pencil strokes explore jungles,

scale graphite mountains where volleys
of mountain men wield black powder rifles,

enter the caves of whimsical dragons
that curl around uncertain treasure.

Now come the Noggas. Bald, baggy creatures
who sit atop telephone poles, need a shave, smoke cigars.

Soon he will sketch his vision, miscalculate,
begin again, draw his own conclusions;

Noggas, like hovering angels, perched on his bedposts.

MONET'S GARDEN AT VETHEUIL

1880, Oil on Canvas
National Gallery of Art, Washington D.C.
Claude Monet, 1840 – 1926

A small child, I glimpsed an instant
of infinity, followed the thought
along, speeding past stars and galaxies
until I feared I would travel forever—
disappear.

Now this young boy frocked in blue,
cornsilk hair, child of sky and garden,
stands on a shadowed path surrounded
by sunflowers; seed orbs like planets,
sprouting golden flames.

Does he ask the artist-father where the path
leads? What is beyond what's seen?
What makes the sky so irresistibly blue
you want to wing into its nothingness,
sure you will find an answer?

The young know about questions.
They know how to fly beyond boundaries,
how beauty rises from the earth,
makes light into a whisper
of blue shadows.

From

NIGHT BEYOND BLACK
2016

CAFÉ TERRACE AT NIGHT

1888, Oil on Canvas
Kroller-Muller Museum, Otterlo, Netherlands
Vincent Van Gogh, 1853 - 1890

Patrons cluster in sulfurous light
while he memorizes darkness, makes it bearable,
emerging, as he did, from gloomy Dutch interiors,
potato fields' dark furrows.

A night painting without black,
with nothing but beautiful blue and violet
and green, the strokes fall heavy,
at right angles to each other,

as if to make sense of that endless sky
where the stars wear coronas—
minor angels calling
to his upturned soul.

A cobbled road, like an uneven
life, leads away, bordered
by empty tables and chairs
just at the edge of light.

Remember the sunflowers' golden glow,
wheat ripening in a summer field,
heat that rises beneath troubled skies.
Nothing could stop those whorls of wild

blackbirds.

DAYBREAK

The morning air is all awash with angels.
~*Richard Wilbur*

The morning air so still,
the birds have stopped to listen,

the rustlings of night creatures
becalmed by dawn's measured light,

and the moon, which filled
Crockett Lake with the face of night,

gives way to daybreak's stealth, a corrugated
shimmer across the surface of the lake.

Fresh from the drone of dreams,
one scene lingers, oozes out of its hive.

My cloak, the exact magenta of sunrise,
streams behind me

as I run down curved stone steps
moving against the wind.

I can't say whether I'm fleeing
or advancing. In dreams, as in life,

one may never know. Poised
at the edge of morning's approaching

light, I see the kingfisher in stationary
position above the lake.

It prepares for the dive.

EROTICA IN UPTOWN

Port Townsend, Washington

Floured footprints lead us down a side street
to the door—*Pane d' Amore.*

Inside, croissants curl against each other
like familiar bed partners.

Currant scones rest side by side,
focaccia nudges Swedish limpa,

ciabatta reclines near mounded rounds,
braided loaves, love-knots—steamy,

yeasty-breathed, and those perky baguettes
that flare like lust from a wicker basket.

I stare until it seems rude; twisted exhibitionists
stacked high against the back wall,

and the sugary brazen ones closer
under glass—blatantly beautiful loaves

kneaded, pressed, stroked, patted,
shaped by clever hands.

Outside on the bench, curved like the curve
of his arm, in flickering sunlight

beneath the ginkgo tree, we watch
people come and go, cradling warm loaves

close to their bodies, all anticipatory
inspiration, and we feed each other

apple croissants sprinkled
with cinnamon and sugar.

LUNCHEON ON THE GRASS

1862-1863, Oil on Canvas
Musée d'Orsay, Paris, France
Edouard Manet, 1832-1883

And didn't you know
it would end like this

in a glade by the river
your clothes puddled nearby

the outrage the scandal
your unrepentant gaze

like the river's constant glide
toward open water

Try to halt
the wheel of seasons

or a seed waiting in the desert
fifty years to bloom with rain

the rain all glint and silent touch
Think of the precarious dewdrop

clinging to a web
that catches morning light

You bring the river with you
beaded silver on your naked skin

drying in the open air

YESTERDAY'S LIGHT

We keep coming back to what we gave up.
~Lisel Mueller

So strong, this impulse
to find the exact spot
near the swinging bridge
where the country store once stood.

The empty field owes me nothing.
I drive by slowly, follow
the river road and memories:
dark oiled floors, the fragrance
of blueberry buckle fresh
from the oven, a plump little woman,
housedress and apron, who stepped
from behind a curtained doorway,
scooped peach ice cream
on a summer day,
sunlight muted through the maple.

This need to travel back
to find that depot of innocence.
The fifties steak house,
white and chrome and black,
its green awning long gone
the building now splashed
with garish red and yellow script
in a language I don't understand.
Near the heavy entrance door
I close my eyes, smell gardenia,
my prom date corsage,
picture the boy who pinned it on,
his eyes soft like brown velvet.

At the end of Main Street,
the fountain replaced
with a more efficient rotary,
stained glass windows
removed from the Spanish-style
church where, long ago,
friends gathered
to witness our wedding vows.

Now an arrow points
to the upper floor
and a neon sign flashes
in one of the clear window panes:
Tattoo Parlor—
the needle-prick of now,
the indelible imprint of then.

SHE TURNED FIFTY

Have you ever noticed?
Barbie always walks
on tiptoes,
mincing along
as if sneaking
up on Ken,
a flat-footed dude,
able to get
where he wants to go,
never mind what's
expected of him.
Only by wearing
spike heels
does she achieve
balance.
Hobbled
as she is
by her
acutely
angled shoes,
she lacks
mobility
to run away
from
her not
so
perfect
life.

TILT

Sometimes I forget
how the earth spins and tilts,

shifts its tectonic plates
causing the ground to split

and groan and tremble.
How sun storms throw

radioactive darts in our direction
and burning boulders skim

the atmosphere. The rose window
high in the gable of our seaside

home records the sun's arc
and the moon's advances.

Its mullions split sunlight,
a shadowy web

that slips down the wall,
its morning tracery spread across

the floor capturing the rhythm
and swirl of our staggering days.

On moonlit nights, beams of light
pour through the window's

openings arranged in changing
curves and triangles, a rotation

I trust, forgetting I walk
on particles amassed around

a molten core, suspended
from nothing.

GARDEN PRANKS

For Brian

Do you remember?
Sleeping beneath the night sky
declaring, with the confidence
of a three-year-old, the moon is my friend.

Morning visits to the garden,
you loosened the grip of the bean tendrils,
spiraled the plants around their poles
in the opposite direction trying to convince
them, against spin and pull of the earth,
they could choose their own way.

A robin's egg found on moss beneath the fir tree,
color of pure turquoise, a treasure you longed
to possess, but did not touch.

I wanted to give you the moon
so you would never feel alone.
I wanted you to know one almost
always has choices, and that some things
are so precious you touch them
only with your heart
and a lifetime of memories.

WHERE POEMS WINTER

I settle into a packed barrel of dreams.
Staves hold the gleaming apples in,

a hole near the bottom lets juice
run out. Here truth ferments:

a yellow barn rises, yes flies
above a sapphire lake,

an orchid, pressed between pages
of an ancient book renewed by dew,

bees that touch and spin
words into a saffron cord,

a pen trapped and scribbling
in the corner of a blank page

like a swallow that enters an open
window, now desperate for sky.

TAMARACK

I travel east into the Cascades
to a small town my parents
came to as newlyweds,

follow double yellow lines,
the road too treacherous for passing,
search for a small cabin

where I was conceived. More gold
than yellow, the center lines
mimic the hue of autumn tamarack

released of its evergreen pretensions.
The tamaracks flare
above a scud of clouds

draped over the valley,
rise
toward snow-topped peaks.

Carried out of these mountains
curled like a leaf
in my mother's womb,

I unfurled in a different place.
Return is like seeing the negative
from a long time ago,

a bright image that remains
for an instant
after you close your eyes.

EAST OF THE MOUNTAINS

For Fran

You know the disposition of grief,
how it bends you like wheat,
an undulating field of waves,
swept by a searing wind.

How it twists what you know
to be true, not from lack
of kindness, but because
it knows no other way.

Grief comes disguised in blue
so intense it seems black,
but remember that tender time
in the spring, before summer's heat

dictates the landscape,
how morning dew lingers
in sheltered places and wild violets
flourish in the valley.

CASCADE SUITE

What overcomes him,
causes him to stop
at this particular place
west of Rainy Day Pass
near the Pacific Crest Trail?

Is it the resinous scent
coaxed from Grand fir and hemlock
by summer sun,

the jade river sliding
like ruched silk over a bed of stones,

the mists of waterfalls that spin
blue and violet prisms
above salal and Oregon grape,
asters and lupine falling
like an amen on the skin?

Is it imagined echoes
poised to bounce from the granite
slabs and ravines of Liberty Bell,
Mount Fury, and The Prophet,

or mountain air
so pure there is no choice
but song?

I see him briefly as we flash
by in our car.

Pulled off to the side of the road,
he perches on the tailgate of a truck,
French horn pressed against his lips,
tucked into his arms like a new bride.

WITHOUT NOTICE

Oak Harbor, Washington

Sometimes loss announces its intentions,
other times it arrives suddenly, without notice.

I learned Easter Sunday that it was gone—
the Garry oak that had made peace with the sky

for three hundred thirty years. It once defined
the corner of my great-uncle's property,

a favorite uncle who was generous with kisses
and home-grown beefsteak tomatoes.

It had been felled early one morning, I was told,
by those who deemed it dangerous.

Loss creeps around the edges of helplessness
and we are like songbirds who have lost their

shelter and exuberant songs.

BREATHE

Frightened, we hold
our breath, but that's not
what happened.

That summer day at the lake,
so young, no reason
to think about consequences.

Sifting my mother's care
through my fingers was as easy
as breathing. Near the shore

a water slide. Ten steps up,
that irresistible curvy swish
to the bottom. I had asked again

and again. Been told, *No. Someday
when you're a better swimmer,*
yet I was drawn to that shiny

chute the way light glints
off a silver coin and strikes
the eye of a crow.

From the top of the slide,
this scaffold of independence,
I saw my mother resting

on the shore and quickly launched
myself down—such a perfect forbidden
glide. In an instant I slipped

into the blue-green water
as smoothly as a button
through its loop,

surprised I could not find
my footing. I watched shimmering
bubbles escape and rise,

curious observer of a strange
pale light, a dreamy underwater world
where I floated, not knowing

I had slid off the edge
of all that was safe
and predictable.

BIOPSY

The first slice of day is best.
I choose the largest piece.

This last morning of summer,
the perennial garden rain-faded,

the fields greening toward winter,
a road crew's chain saw cuts

the crust of silence, clearing away
the willow that fell in a sudden

summer storm, an untimely
squall carrying more force

because it found us unaware,
changed the familiar landscape

in an instant to something
distant, unrecognizable.

How trusting we were that morning
as we raised the first cups of coffee

to our lips, thinking everything
would remain the same.

WHAT WE REMEMBER

This morning, watching how the sun
pours through the slats of the arbor,

infuses the air with the scent
of honeysuckle, I step into the yard

and find a four-point buck
not ten feet away.

He considers me intently
as I do him and I wonder...

I go back to the house, cut an apple
into slices and return.

He comes to me without hesitation
and, one by one, takes each slice

from my hand. Yes, I'm quite certain
this is the little buck I fed those years ago

when the antler buds had not yet
blossomed, here at this exact spot

in my garden; the little buck that nudged
my hand, impatient for more apple.

Now the imposing presence of that great
rack rising and dipping as he eats,

his breath warm on my hand, the muscled
nearness of his wide chest and shoulders—

two creatures with a history
of trust, and in his eyes an understanding

as quiet and sure as a guiding star.

THIS MOMENT OF GRACE

Alone on the street of a small town,
I walk toward the light of a bakery

where young people work late
shaping *stollen* for Christmas tables,

and the full moon hangs its silence
in my heart. The crisp winter night

arranges thoughts scattered like stars
into sharp focus, a perfect moment

that will ripen to memory.
Who can say what makes it so?

Like an authentic image captured
when the subject is unaware,

I see my life without smudges,
blurs, or margins, and in that instant

I understand. I have always
felt well loved.

WINTER STILLNESS

Crockett Prairie, Whidbey Island

Light from the window angles
across the snow-laden field,
soundless flakes building
upon themselves
like small-parceled
courage.

The snow glows, covers rabbit hole,
the runs of vole, as dusk deepens,
edges into the forest, a dark sweep
of purple that silences bird call
and the skittering of small
brave creatures.

Venus billows from the bell
of the moon, icy light riveting
darkness, striking the willow,
wild rose thicket, and evergreen
boughs now fatigued
with snow.

It's what we do not hear
that makes us listen: the space
between words breathing
what is unspeakable, the pause
between heartbeats that still
has rhythm.

ALMANAC

My grandparents owned the land,
worked the land, bound
to the earth by seasons of planting
and harvest.

They watched the sky, the habits
of birds, hues of sunset,
the moods of moon and clouds,
the disposition of air.
They inhaled the coming season,
let it brighten their blood
for the work ahead.

Soil sifted through their fingers,
imbedded beneath their nails,
and this is what they knew:
this rhythm circling the years.
They never left their land—
each in their own time
settled deeper.

WHEN SILENCE WAS ENOUGH

For My Father

Not the sort of silence that falls with snow,
nor the interlude between heartbeats;

more the musical pattering of raindrops—
the things we say to each other

barely penetrating the surface. Questions unasked
leave a mineralized vein of history

and more than that, nuggets of a life unclaimed
on a stream bed of everyday conversation.

Evenings, returning from work, he splashed
the tiredness from his face, water going beyond

where it was expected, a fountain of exuberance,
and we held out our hands to catch the drops.

The happy child, the competent father—
feelings you know to be true only half

the bond. Now questions...
The questions...

What did you dream and what got away?

GREEN '58 CHEVY APACHE TRUCK

The only time I saw my father cry
was when our dog died.

The call came early Sunday morning,
heart too weak to withstand surgery.

Mac, our boxer, runt of the litter,
grew tall and stately, chest blazed

in white. He loved to ride
in the passenger seat of my father's

pickup, like two like teenagers
on a first date. They were a familiar pair,

joyriding around our small town,
Mac nudging ever closer

until he could lean against my father,
both of them behind the wheel.

After my father put down the phone
that morning, he said he needed

to be gone for a while.
Drove away in the truck.

CURRICULUM VITAE

After Lisel Mueller

The day I was born my parents labored:
my mother for obvious reasons,
my father to expel a kidney stone.

Gloom of the Great Depression behind them,
the glare of war in their eyes,
my parents gave me a hero's welcome.

Quiet times on the farm. Buttercups,
bleeding hearts, barn cats, lady bugs,
learning to cope with a happy childhood.

Afternoons, reading in the moss-covered
junction of a huge maple tree,
I found the shelter and bliss of words.

A hospital was my classroom:
the cosmic echo of a newborn's first cry,
the unbroken silence of the departed.

A deep, quixotic voice led me to an altar
of promises, nights of burning stars, the two-part
invention of sons, a breathless rush of years.

Stacking lumber to build a home, nails buried deep
in safety, contentment. Ordinary moments
that sparked and glowed.

Then loss and more loss. Lost in a dark forest
of grief. Compassion held out its hand
and I hung on.

The hurt of beauty, an indefinable longing,
recommended me to poetry. Steady work,
polishing the cells of the hive

to receive the sweetness.

HOMAGE TO PLATT ROGERS SPENCER

It mattered then, strokes
as elegant as butterfly wings.
Loops and scrolls inked
on pages of yearbooks,
birth certificates, bank contracts
and everyday posts—envelopes,
recipe cards, and twining
down grocery lists.

It twirled away at the end
of a signature, returning to underline
the given and inherited, a definition
of lightness born more of respect
than vanity.

We sat at little oak desks, hooked
to each other like railroad cars
and practiced the Palmer Method,
loops perfectly coiled
as though they might spring
off the page.

Now, time is our master.
Calls, emails, texts sliding off
the tip of a swirling whip,
all shockingly similar missives
that strike with a staccato beat.

Down by the road, the old-fashioned
mailbox waits. Amid a flurry
of bills and ads, occasionally
a hand-written letter. Opening
the letter's envelope is like slipping
between sheets dried in an island breeze.

Further down the road an islander
has painted her mailbox tea rose pink.
On the side, in lovely Spencerian
script, her simple directive:
Love Letters Only.

DOING DISHES

She said she had always wanted to do it—
throw away dirty dishes rather than wash them,

and she did, after breakfast, toss the blue, green,
orange, and yellow Fiestaware into the trash.

Transferring from New York to Germany
with her husband and children,

the movers coming that day, she chucked the dishes
in among banana peels, egg shells, coffee grounds,

bits of bacon, paper towels, and called it good.
What she could not know is that a young mother

in that very town received a much needed set
of tableware when her husband returned

home from work that evening: bright dishes
that showed up chipped and grubby

like old friends with egg on their faces.

CHOICES WE MAKE WHEN WE ARE
TOO YOUNG TO MAKE THEM

Evenings at the table with my father,
stewing over algebraic equations,

chemical reactions, my young life
sloped toward science and healing.

He didn't recognize, nor did I,
how I fingered letters

the way the devout touch
prayer beads, that I held them

up to my ear to hear the music
they made when strung together,

a child rearranging alphabet blocks,
balancing them into a fragile

tower that spelled out something
I was too young to understand.

I can't say how we know
we please without hearing the exact

words, but I knew. His pride in me
slipped into my hands with soup spoons

and Yardley's soap as I fed and bathed him
during the last months of his life.

I often wonder if he is surprised,
living as he does, in the spaces

between words, there among
the pages of my books.

TESTIMONY OF RAIN

The storm rants through the Strait
of Juan de Fuca, many voices
threatening, yet exhilarating,
this dark night, as it sweeps
breakers onshore, batters
the stand of twisted evergreens.
How to distinguish where one sound
ends, another begins; a mash
of sky and sea, the thrashing
arms of trees.

The storm unravels its ball of fury
and moves on. Now the syncopated
dance of raindrops on the cabin
roof, a voice that repeats a familiar
childhood story. When did my young
life end, this one begin?

I remember one moment, my son
home from college, the two of us
walking together in soft rain.
He puts his arm around me, pulls me
into a deep puddle. Holding hands,
we jump up and down,
splashing like demented toddlers.

SUBMERGED

A flotilla of mergansers floats by on an outgoing tide,
their reflections splayed on the blue-green water.
They duck below the surface of the bay, disappear,
pop up nibbling on small fish.

How would it feel to disappear, if only for a moment,
dip below the surface of a life, go deep
to find what truly nourishes,
and if we were to look back at the reflection
left in the world, would it be beautiful?

From

GLINT
2019

THE THEORY OF EVERYTHING

If everything's connected, I want to be

the green of a leopard's eye. I want to be

a snowflake, among other snowflakes,

each unique, poised on the bareness

of a winter branch. I want to be

the glint of light on a summer wave,

a speck of salt in a tear of joy,

the giggle of a small boy playing

in a puddle of mud. I want to be

the space between notes in the intermezzo

of Mascagni's opera, the fragrance

of lilac in the spring.

If everything's connected, I want to be

a striation of muscle in your beating heart.

FLIGHT PATH

I hear them before I see them,
raucous excitement coming from the north

and I run out to witness dark approaching clouds
that splinter into familiar aerodynamic chevrons:

the wild geese, waves and waves of them,
cresting over the house toward the lake at dusk.

Is it their fidelity to the season that lifts us up
to meet them, as if we are being birthed

into new expectations? Maybe we don't need to know
of the magnetic pull that directs them toward the poles

or the landmarks they remember
from earlier journeys. I like the mystery;

stars beginning to prick the deep of night,
winged silhouettes against the full moon.

MIRABILIA

A question no one can seem to answer.
What's to be done with beauty?

A sweep of melody that lifts to the crest
of weeping. The colors of water

swirling below Deception Pass Bridge,
hues so pure yet elusive.

The light and shine of satin in a Singer Sargent
painting—too much to take in; it spills

from a vessel of gratitude. Sunlight on the inlet
as it flashes toward night,

like a mythological sequined fish breaking
waves into strands of silver and gold.

The cinnamon, nutmeg, and clove fragrance
of apple butter simmering all day in a heavy pot.

A quivering dewdrop on the cusp of autumn
that clings to the tatting of a spider's web.

What's to be done? I cannot hold these things
nor let them go.

RIPE SEASON

Picking blueberries and I think
there is a poem here, but I can't find it.
The sun is warm. I shade my eyes, peer
through foliage dense and summer green.

Fat blueberries hang in tight clusters.
Their wild beauty springs from high
mountain meadows; the berries,
now cultivated in my garden,
even when baked into pancakes, muffins,
and pies, cannot be tamed. They burst,
spilling unrestrained flavor upon the tongue.

The green ones, tight and unyielding,
lack sweetness and I ponder this, pledging
to loosen my grip on preconceived notions.

My pail fills as ripe blueberries,
like miniature moons the color of twilight,
fall into my palm.

NOVEMBER

November's leaves have slipped
their mooring. Now they belong
to the wind and rain and earth.

Once glowing among evergreens
like eyes of the wild, they collect
in sodden masses against curbs

and over the grates of storm drains.
There is nothing to recommend
them, their beauty sacrificed
to the work of the season.

The necessary letting go
of things past to herald
another cycle.

Now we look to the sculptural
shapes of unadorned trees
against a winter sky,

simplicity its own beauty.

FOG

There is something mysterious about fog.
It whispered to Sandburg as it crept into the harbor

on little cat feet. It settles over Admiralty Inlet,
a downy comforter of relief on a simmering summer day.

It moves in quickly, a cool mist that settles lightly
on our faces and arms as we trudge up the hill

toward home. Then the stillness, how it tamps down
sound, reminding us to honor silence and drift

through an inner landscape of ideas,
enter into the ethereal magic of another world

as if we were birds soaring in clouds
that have come down to enfold us,

quieting the minor furies we create.

WOLF MOON

The January moon is ripe. It spills its light
into the dark night, an extrovert needing to be
the center of attention. There is a reason
wolves howl when the moon reveals the fullness
of itself, and although I haven't done so,
I've felt the urge—a longing so ancient and wild
as if in a time past we came from an enchanted place,
a place so beautiful we want only to return.

Now the moon casts its cold white light
onto everything—fields glitter and the lake
gives itself up to receive the radiance
of that dominating presence.

We may lose ourselves in brilliance,
an attraction that smolders, just waiting to be lit.
No secrets, no dark and quiet corners.
The moon demands clarity.

Come into the light.

A SMALL POEM ABOUT SOMETHING BIG

I've long thought it's all about light.
How it persists, creeps under closed doors,
rises each morning to defeat darkness.

It seeps from the full moon,
a silver drizzle across the face
of Crockett Lake,

and is there in my beloved's eyes
at the beginning of each day,
a beacon that guides me to what is true.

Babies, those angels of light—
we are blinded by the flare
of their smiles, of who they are.

An irresistible light leads people
on a final journey, and now, scientists
working with in vitro fertilization,

have seen microscopic sparks
of light at the exact moment
of conception.

ALL OF IT

Too much has been said of love and not enough.
How to speak of inner tides, light on a restless sea.

Fog, obscure and quiet, drifts in without warning,
dampens the bell buoy's distant clanging.

We nibble at the edges of love's mystery
replete, yet forever starved.

We are like mariners without charts,
scribes without pens.

A moonflower blooms in darkness.
A dragonfly rests with open wings.

Shattered glass forms the mosaic's design,
and swallows gather before parting.

All of it, all of it—salt and light.
Solving the mystery is as futile as trying

to steal a fingerprint.

THE QUIET ONE

Somehow, it is difficult to write about my mother.
Although she's been gone for many years,
it is as if the closeness we shared
cannot be shared with others.

A patient, quiet woman, she never spanked
or uttered criticism. Do we ever know
how much we're loved?

On cold winter mornings, she warmed my clothes
by the stove before helping me dress for school,
and I remember a cabled sweater with pearl buttons
she knitted for me.

Her gentleness flowed to her grandchildren
and as they got older, they teased her about how
she always ran to answer the phone on the first ring.

Hers was a subtle strength. In times of adversity she said,
You do what you have to do. As I left home, a reminder,
You are responsible for your own happiness.

That is all I can tell you, for now, about my mother.
What she gave me is like knowing when the tide goes out
it will always come back in.

SMALL TOWN COFFEE HOUSE

We don't know what to do.

We look at each other through a scrim of silence,

finger the thin hem of our understanding,

feel the frayed edge of heartbreak.

After the fog turned hard, after the shriek of steel,

the glitter of glass shards on the rain-slick road,

the hush of it everywhere.

How are we left with nothing but silence?

She didn't know when she left for work

that morning she would not arrive,

the young barista who always smiled

as she steamed our espressos

and the thing is,

I didn't know her name.

IMPROVISATION

*...sometimes it is the artist's task to find out how much music
you can still make with what you have left.*
          ~Itzhak Perlman

It was reported he said this following a concert
at Lincoln Center after a string snapped on his violin.

He continued playing, at one with his music;
notes, like holy sparks, rose and spiraled

into the bodies and psyches of those in the audience.
The sweat, the tears amid cheers, the standing ovation.

Call it a gift of improvisation or simple perseverance.
And don't we all know the lesson here?

Aren't we all broken?

It doesn't matter if the story is true. Every day
is a growing season.

We can nourish ourselves on the richness of the quote.
Our task is to make music with what remains.

STRANGE BEDFELLOWS

We don't belong to the night, nor it to us.
Its hospitality erratic, we enter through a curious
portal not knowing if we will descend into a deep
canyon of rest or a cave of winged terror.

Random events pull us back to forgotten pasts,
while our imaginations paint astonishing
scenes on the walls of our slumber.

Sleep, a drama like the half-darkened
face of Lady Macbeth, a mystery
that plays out again and again.

Frequent visitors, we willingly submit
to its paralyzing darkness, give ourselves
completely, with every assurance
we will return to the light.

PRAYER

Father, I am weary of the division in the world. The clang
of dissension, the clamor of estrangement and alienation.

A meadow filled with sunlight calls, and autumn light
softens the cottonwoods' golden furies as they shadow
the river. Doves released from the dovecote fly
their freedom. They turn in unison, an exquisite unfurling
that blesses sky.

I don't want to be one who turns away from ugliness
and the need that underlies it all, but the world
is splintered and what good comes of gathering kindling
only to build fires that burn cold?

Don't we all want to find our own understanding, come
to our own conclusions, and why do we think, for one
instant, we could do that for another?

For now, I will seek the communion of flowers,
how the peony opens up to receive light
and the lily-of-the-valley whispers, *You must also learn
to live in the shade.*

ST. MARY'S AUTUMN RUMMAGE SALE

This must be the light artists in the south of France
crave, how everything seems supercharged—
spun gold luster that gilds oaks and evergreens,
asters and hydrangeas, an intimacy of air and light.
I feel a quiet yet sudden change, as the tectonic plate
of autumn slides over a weary summer.

We walk past St. Mary's, see a throng of people
stretching from its doors out to the road.
A lot of people needing confession, my husband jokes.
A lot of sinning going on, a passerby responds.

We see the priest blessing the shoppers as they enter
the church. Outside, the wind, that old prophet of autumn,
comes to claim its followers, leaves twirling, falling,
skittering along the road like brown-robed monks.

CONFESSIONS OF A YEASAYER

I feel as if I'm in the turbulence the ferry makes
when the prop reverses, approaching the landing—
stirred up and restless, easily annoyed by almost
everyone and everything.

As a woman who normally sees the best in others,
elevates them to unattainable heights,
for the present, I'm glimpsing a few folks
in The Emperor's New Clothes, silly and unattractive.

It's not as if I'm on a lonely journey to nowhere,
but after a week of others piling on, all minor offenses,
I'm feeling the need for comfort and retreat.

I luxuriate in my favorite bookstore, there among the stacks
of poetry, the shelves so high I need a stepstool to reach the top.
Tottering in the dusty loftiness of bliss, I sneeze.

From one stack over I hear, *Bless you*. I chuckle and say,
Thank you. Another sneeze, another *Bless you*. Wow,
twice blessed. Wonder if I could do this on demand.

I ponder the benefits, a book of Kumin essays in my hand.
Sometimes life is like a sneeze. The build-up, a minor
explosion, a sudden release of irritants, the return

to normal, and amazingly you breathe easily once again.

SMALL TOWN SATURDAY NIGHT

Hamburgers at our local eatery, a funky tavern that sports a moose head wearing a baseball cap, a toilet seat suspended from the ceiling, dusty photos of movie stars who ate here when *Practical Magic* was filmed in our town, and as you leave, a slanted wooden floor that makes you feel as if you have had more to drink than you have. Jaywalking across one of the two blocks of our main street, a SUV pulls up, a window opens, a blonde middle-aged woman, clearly in a heightened state of excitement, calls to us—*Chocolate Night in Coupeville*, holds out a plastic container filled with Hersey's Dark Chocolate Kisses. We each grab one, unwrap and eat without a moment of hesitation. *We may drop dead before we reach home*, my husband says, but hey, happiness is where you find it.

SEPTEMBER

One afternoon
summer measures its hem
and finds it has outgrown
its season, even now, shadows
falling toward autumn. It covers
its ears, refuses to hear
the skein of wild geese
unraveling in the sky
and how the wind churns
the willow's leaves, a faint
chatter like seeds shaken
in a dried-out gourd.
The air's moist expectancy
confirms what we know
to be true: the textures
and dimensions of change.
Choice stitches us to the comfort
of the familiar, or snips
the threads that bind us
to what we have outgrown.

THE FAR EDGE OF LONGING

Photograph by Emily Gibson

I keep going back to it. I don't know why
I'm so attracted to the photo of a dandelion
at its time of ripeness. Beyond the exquisite,
delicate beauty of the seed head,
there is something more.

Something about a seed partially detached
from the fragile orb, waiting for passage
to an unknown destination, the wind
an ancient conveyance.

Something about the slender shaft, the seed
poised at the tip like the point of a tiny arrow,
and the feathery fibers at the opposite end,
a miniature parachute set for descent.

Something about the potential of this humble
tuft of fluff uniquely prepared to be planted
in the place it belongs.

I imagine how it would feel to be lifted up,
carried away in the arms of the wind.
To drift in random flight, the allure
of not knowing how or when or where.

NEBULOSITY

Blue Moon, March 31, 2018

In the country, night becomes a deep well of darkness.
Coyotes howl success or disappointment; owls, those silent
missiles, aim at scuttering mice and rabbits
with deadly precision.

When my young grandson visits from the city, he says,
The stars are closer at your house, Nana, the Big Dipper tipped
to offer a cup of cool water, other stars winking, spilling
champagne, bubbles floating in a darkened sky.

This celebration of vastness, those distant counselors,
beacons, guiding us to mystery beyond ourselves.
They say love speaks with light. I will hold onto what I know,
mindful of what we can never know.

Tonight, a blue moon adds its radiance, overflows
across the lake. Like thirsty wanderers, we drink the light
yet are never full.

From

ROAD SIGNS AND HOBO MARKS
2020

SONG FOR THE ROAD

A good traveler has no fixed plans
and is not intent on arriving.
~Lao-Tzu

Travelers tote a portable definition
of home. It is scribbled in the dust
of the road, embedded in light
that slants through shuttered forests,
and comes unbidden in the call
of a distant train.

It quivers just beyond
the next expectation, shimmers
over the river's smocked surface
unspooling down a mountainside
under a mood of clouds.

Caught in the reflective flash
of city windows and a skyline etched
against a setting sun,

it is chalked in alleyways,
and on the gatepost of a stranger's
rural home.

Sojourners adopt the comfort
of the road, the communal warmth
of campfire, while on a bosky hillside
the red-eyed towhee scruffs up the earth,
a primal dance, as if worshipping
the thrill of an ancient flame.

THE GREAT DEPRESSION

President Hoover says, *About the time*
we think we can make ends meet,
someone moves the ends.

Faces lined with hopelessness,
an unfamiliar scrawl that connects
men gathered around a soup kettle.
Kids in tattered clothes roll a discarded
tire rim down a dusty road; a woman slumps
on the curb, head cupped in her hands.

Marchers carry signs, *We want to be citizens*
not transients. Woody Guthrie sings
Going Down the Road Feeling Bad.

These flinty people somehow
pull themselves up, in spite of despair,
the way some save tiny pieces of string,
tie pieces together to make
something useful.

HOBO PRIDE

Like a dousing stick that seeks water,
a hobo rides the rails to find work,

unlike the tramp who travels and works
only when forced to do so,

or the bum who does not travel
and does not work.

Their glyphs, a uniform code chalked
on light poles and fence posts,

aid those who follow: where to find
clean water, safe lodging, a kind heart.

They meet every August in Britt, Iowa, a family
of travelers who speak the same language.

Musicians and storytellers gather around
a common fire, celebrate their oneness.

The poets among them understand
how the mouth of night exhales its vapors

and how frost makes the dahlia beautiful
before it dies.

MEANING OF A NAME

Some choose a life on the road,
for others no luxury of choice.
Oldest son in a Depression family,
too many mouths to feed,
sent off to his fate on the road.

This boy of twelve, skinny child,
homeless boy—*a hobo*, stares
into the ominous face of survival.

There is no point for me to pivot on,
so protected my entire life.
I can't hear the crunch of the road,
the rumble of an empty belly.

What of this child? My imaginings
leave him scuffing down the road,
drinking from a spring
of disappointment, hungry always
for the warmth of a kitchen,
the shelter of familiar arms.

He will stake a claim to independence,
wade through need to grasp
a hand of goodwill,
learn the new language
of aloneness.

SHELTER

We can only know
the truth of our own story.

I have not traveled the boulevards
of your desires, been seduced

by the rhythm of wheels on rails,
or the murmur of a dark river.

Home always beyond
the next curve in the road

and work what you find,
where you find it.

I can imagine the comfort
of this symbol: two wavy lines

supported by a straight, vertical stroke,
a small circle sheltered underneath.

Rest in a barn loft filled with fresh hay
that smells of summer.

Hear rain's patter, watch lightning
flash through cracks in the walls.

The cows have been milked,
now quiet in their stalls.

Their breath warms the space
with a grassy vapor.

Morning opens to pale washed light
and the rooster's fanatical gladness.

Now cow bells and the clanking
of milk pails—a brief contentment.

A barn cat curls at your feet, wanting
only the comfort of a warm body.

EXTENDED FAMILY

They always set an extra place at their dinner table
for drop-in friends or unexpected guests.

One afternoon, just before dinner, a man came by
asking if he could work for food.

My friend and the traveling man raked leaves
that littered the front yard.

Afterwards, clean up at the sink and an invitation
to dinner; the guest served first.

No prying, just everyday conversation.
As he put on his coat to leave, tears watered

the furrows of his weathered face. *Can't remember
when I've had a hot meal like that, let alone*

sat at a table with family. They never saw him again.
He came into their lives like the wild geese that signal

untamed change. We are attracted to their call,
and charmed by the rightness of their sure flight.

ON THE EDGE

Danger crouches in the corners of boxcars
and in the clattering space between wheels and track.

It escapes over the lip of a bottle
to the lips of a desperate wanderer,

snarls from the throats of bone polishers
and menacing, angry men.

It glints off the edge of a knife's blade,
skips along a pitchfork's tines.

Hobos, carrying only bindle sticks, face the hard
fist of winter, the searing slap of summer's temper.

Inhaling risks, they measure the next breath
as testament to another day.

Finally, in remembrance, hobos who carry on,
tap their walking sticks on the gravestones

of those who have *caught the westbound*.

BURLAP

*Armbands made of burlap are worn by those
in attendance at a hobo memorial service.*

Not the patterned elegance of moiré,
nor satin's ballroom glow.
Common and coarse as a charwoman's
hands or a line-dried towel.

Here the touch of a callused palm
caught in the feedbag's weave;
burlap raised to the horse's mouth,
filled with the grain of truth.

Potatoes lifted from earth's dark closet
shed their dusty layers, hibernate
inside burlap's sturdy shelter.

Burlap belongs to rivers and fields
and everyday people. Tattered and earthy,
it challenges our ideas of beauty, and wraps
our roots in what is real.

THE BONE POLISHER

Bad Dog lives in our neighborhood.
That's his name: Bad Dog, a basset hound.

He's not bad, really, just kind of dumb.
My grandson and I installed a night vision camera

and placed piles of meat scraps, hoping to photograph
coyotes that hunt nightly in our fields.

In the morning a flashing red light indicates
photographs have been taken.

Captured on the camera: fifteen photos
of Bad Dog, eating all the meat.

Hobos need not worry about a threat
from Bad Dog. No need here to place a symbol,

that looks vaguely like teeth, to warn
followers of a *mean dog, a bone polisher.*

I wish only that my home be marked
with a smiling cat:

A kindhearted lady lives here.

HARD SCRABBLE LIFE

Ruth Stone, 1915–2011

Ruth Stone stalks truth. She writes
of a hard scrabble life *stained with pokeberries.*
She lived on *greens and back-fat and biscuits.*

The closest I can get to that life is my recipe
for Hobo Bread, a concoction of farm ingredients
baked in tin cans as hobos did during the Depression.

Poet dear, I'm inspired by your gnarly hands
grubbing stumps off your back forty, how you would
run when the words came, back to the cabin

to catch them before they got away. You took them
as they were, in grimy overalls, dirt under
their fingernails, bruised and wounded.

The hobos would have loved you, sitting around
a campfire, chewing the fat, an unlikely queen
proffering such naked, elegant words.

DEAR BO

I don't think you wish for wings.
I imagine your footsteps find ease
in the permanence of earth,
gravel's crunch, and the chuffing
sound of mud.

You persist in my mind and I,
like a pileated woodpecker, drum
my head against the questions
of your need.

The obvious: to go where there is work,
but what of the enchantment of the road?
Does it circulate in the pathways of your blood?
We all are born crying for release.
When did that become your urgent need?

I don't know when or where this will reach you.
In my dreams, you are a sunflower growing wild
on a Nebraska prairie, then suddenly
you turn into a wolf with kind eyes.

THE CAREGIVER

When my son was in college he picked up a hobo
standing in rain at the edge of the road.

This son, unable to ignore anyone in need, bundled
the shivering man and his crutches into the car

and took him home. After providing a hot shower
and fresh underwear, he soaped and lathered the man's face,

shaved off weeks of growth. He cleaned and dressed
the inflamed stump of the hobo's right leg.

Following supper, the guest bedded down on the couch,
sleeping as if guarded by angels.

Next morning, fitted with a warm winter coat,
the traveler took to the road once again.

Does he hear romance in the call of a distant train?
Is there always a destination or never?

Some know what they need to be happy,
others know what they need to survive.

ROAD SIGNS AND HOBO MARKS

I

How many signs have we missed
and where would we be if we had seen them?

Flares warning accident ahead, caution
and stops obvious to everyone but ourselves.

Arrows that point in opposite directions.
Starting out we venture along by touch and feel,

blind to who we are, what we need.
How could we know?

The young wander in a vast landscape of choice
not knowing they can choose.

II

Soothed by repetition, seasons signal
a certain comfort,

our shadows moving across the years
with the tilt and spin of the earth.

We live within boundaries of change
without rising to its freedoms,

the way pansies lift themselves up
after a sprinkling of water;

too many days knotted into a tangle
of habit and duty.

The silver glint of rain, a certain slant
of light, grasses dried by summer heat,

snowberries and rosehips
primed for celebration.

III

So many signs we miss in our short life span:
The imperceptible movement of glacial ice fields,

explosions and deaths of stars, fossils in eternal sleep.
The universe sings, our time too brief for its melodies

to resolve in a grand finale of understanding.

IV

Deer come daily to my door.
They talk with persuasive eyes.

I cut apples. They eat slices
from my hand. Their wildness

has marked my house
with a language of trust.

Here an easy touch,
sure to find a handout.

Aren't we all beggars?

CHIMACUM

Small community on the Olympic Peninsula

Somewhere a fire is burning.
Someone is tending the fire.

Someone is gathering eggs,
feeding the calves, mucking

out the barn, and near
the crossroads

someone bellies up
to the diner's counter,

coffee sloshing over the rim
of an ironstone mug.

At the community center,
squirrels nip cones from fir trees,

a woodland syncopation
that punctuates the rural stillness.

Everything seems to walk
on soundless feet.

A man moseys along the road
clutching a brown paper bag.

Ordinary, yet remarkable
how we trundle

along each day
balancing our ration

of simple joys,
quiet troubles.

WHAT SOME CALL WILD

Some called him wild,
this young man who became
my father.

Soon after graduation, traveling north
to work and sluice what he could
of life in Alaskan gold fields.

Honeysuckle spiraling
into the forest like wildfire
does not name its wildness,

nor the Nootka rose
which spills sweet wine
from thicket into night air;

even wild mustard
that prances along the fence line
blesses the goldfinch.

How much of wildness
is exuberance
set free?

I hear him in raindrops
that patter on the cabin roof.
It sounds like laughter.

WELLINGTON ON STEVENS PASS

March 1, 1910: ninety-seven passengers and railroad personnel
lost their lives in the worst railroad disaster in U.S. history.

The Great Northern serpentines into the Cascades,
rising and tunneling toward the west coast.

On board a young man travels, request of his parents,
to mediate grief following the death of his wife,

his small child left behind in their care.
He wants only to return.

Two opposing attorneys, unknown to each other,
are bound for the Supreme Court in Olympia.

Another man, estranged from his wife, journeys
west toward reconciliation.

And a widow tends her three children,
having just buried their father—

the infant's greedy need of breast,
toddlers jumping on the green mohair seats.

The train ascends through evergreens crusted
with wings of snow, flakes glitter

in blue dusk, a ballet of ice
swirling in the engine's headlamps.

Passengers dine, they smoke, exchange stories,
soothed by the rhythmic sway of the coach,

the steady click-click of wheels marking time
over steel connections.

They crest the summit, begin descent
until the storm's rage prevents further passage.

Four days, five nights stranded on the side
of the mountain, a mounting loft of snow,

fierce wind, thunder and lightning—a white heat
that casts an eerie incandescent beauty over the scene.

That night as they sleep on a crippled train,
the mountain, burdened with incomprehensible

snow, loses its hold, blasts down
the incline; the roar descends

over grinding boulders, cracking ice fields,
the snap of evergreens. It fills each quiet breath.

Claiming everything in its path, the avalanche
stops only when there is no place left to go.

NOTES FROM A RAIN FOREST

Olympic National Park

By the lake, a finch snatches
a fallen crust of bread, pulls off a crumb,
places it in the mouth of his mate.
He repeats this once again.

These secrets of nature,
how they saturate the inner life,
fueled with contrasts and contradictions
too large to fit the tote of our understanding.

So many ways to be together and apart.
Simplicity is a black beetle that scuttles
off with another; same size, shape,
and shine.

And here, nestled in the moss of the rain forest,
Russla emetica, the sickener, the red-capped
mushroom erupting like passion, a challenge
of risk and beauty.

And what are we to make of the gigantic spruce
that spirals upward, the trunk compressing
under its own weight, eventually to fall,
exploding at the end of its journey.

One can get lost in a green mist
of riddles, the glory and vulnerability
of it all. It's like going so deep
into the forest you forget about sky.

WOODWORKER SPEAKS OF MARRIAGE

The forest opens into a clearing, sunlight
sliding down the deep furrows of ancient Sequoias,
giants rooted here since before the birth of Christ.

I once saw a wedged slice of redwood six feet to its point,
he says. Centuries of history marked in those rings,
a concealed clock chiming time:

Dark Ages, Renaissance, explosions of exploration,
plagues, forest fires, drought.
Beginning growth is rapid, rings widely spaced.

With age, growth slows, rings pressed tight
until there is almost no space and the grain
becomes fine, yet at the center, forever,

the heart remains soft.

YELLOWSTONE PARK, 1948

Memory stalks the years,
a distant traveler scuffing up
the dust of nostalgia—
a handmade Indian doll,
scrolled silver belt buckle,
an Old West saloon,
lightning lassoing the night sky
and I a dusty ten-year-old,
in the back seat of the Plymouth.

That night scrubbed in an old iron tub,
Yardley's English Lavender Soap,
clean pajamas, I hear wind rumpling
the pines, cones plunking
on the shingled roof of the cabin,
smooth log walls, butterscotch gold,
and knots like owl's eyes that see
everything. I remember that night
settled deep in a feather bed,
the line-fresh memory
I've used to measure comfort
for over sixty years—

crisp white sheets.

COUNTERBALANCE

She said she could never have another dog,
so much pain when he died, but what is love
without risk?

I say it is fearsome.
This morning the apple tree droops
under the weight of its fruit

and storm clouds skim over the lake,
heavy and threatening, yet hear the musical
pattering of those first raindrops.

What we cherish is weighted with risk,
and love is funny that way, because
it is also the fulcrum that lifts the burden.

MOUNTAIN MAN IN TIE AND WHITE JACKET

For Bob

My dentist pans for gold.
In Montana, at six thousand feet,
he digs, sifting through granite
and flint; trinkets of millennia,
alert to that mineralized vein
burnished in the stream
of his dreams, the one that,
surprisingly, does not glitter.

Fool's gold, he says
when I bring him a twinkling
stone from my garden and then,
sweet man that he is, smiles,
*Interesting rock to come from
an island.*

He may have packed more gold
into the molars of his patients
than he has packed out
of those hills, but I think
he hankers for Townsend,
that little town where friends
wave and wear cowboy hats,
as he grinds and picks
in the hollow of my tooth;
sluices my mouth with water.

SOURDOUGH

The Jesuit baker, Brother Curry, says
capture wild yeast.

A net? A trap? Kind words?
Just a bit of flour, warm potato water,

and a little honey. Cover loosely.
Three days later

a bubbling, frothing cauldron;
a spongy, ever-shifting mass.

No eye of the newt or toe of frog,
wool of bat, tongue of dog.

Some would say pure chemistry,
yet like an ordinary life

that holds its secrets, I like to think
how sweetness nourishes the cells,

the hidden fermentation that brings
about change, the magic of transformation.

My floured hands knead the dough
in praise of air and lightness

and rising.

DRIFT

Not all those who wander are lost.
~ *J.R.R. Tolkien*

A foggy morning at the shore,
a heron glides out of the mist
floating by on a slim raft of driftwood.

Did dense clouds at the heights
force him to find another way to travel?
This elegant, yet comic, mariner

abandons himself to the wind
and tides, an inventive flight
over water.

Slow ease, perfect balance, deviation
from the norm: a fearless artist
creating a unique design.

Sunlight shimmers through the fog
defying sharp boundaries, a soft blend
of unexpected shapes, unplanned course.

At times we need to drift
to clear our vision. We don't know
what we'll find until we wander.

From

THE LESSON OF PLUMS
2020

FRAGILE WINGS

As long as you have mystery you have health.
~ G. K. Chesterton

They say paradox is the tension between things
that don't make sense.

The big questions of a triune God, the rhythm
of seasons, the distance between the beginning
and the end.

Surrounded by mystery, my mind explores
on fragile wings.

The miracle of bodies—a delicate balance
of hormones and chemistry, impossibly born,
departure to the unknown on a final breath.

The disposition of love—what sets it on its journey,
keeps it trudging through years of joy
and hardship and pain?

What of the muse, the generous midwife, that coaxes
concertos, novels, paintings, to life?

How a baby toddles through the maze of language
and finds a voice.

How the spider, a famed architect, builds
its stunning geometric structure, sets lines
so delicate, yet strong.

How finches know to wait on the garden fence
on the day snap peas push through the soil.

Why a single pink poppy grows in the ditch
along Mossy Rock Road.

I say, live the tension. Let the stories be strange.

DEEP

Listen to the silence. Can you hear
the earth humming its mysterious tune?
Can you feel the vibration of stars,
the pulse of tides?

Scientists probe the silent darkness
of ocean depths. Watery images
float to the surface: schools of glistening
fish, a palette of breathtaking colors.
Strange creatures, disguised
to disappear into their surroundings,
some predatory, others hidden
for self-protection.

Imagine creatures so long in darkness,
no need for eyes. Some blind,
some navigating by their own
bioluminescent light.

Frilled sharks, translucent ghost fish,
twelve-foot spider crab, black dragon
fish, sparkling jewel squid, and delicate
strands of harp sponges.

Profound silence, even when veiled
in darkness, may lead to unexpected
places, an inward journey that invites
us to listen. To go deep is to realize
how much we don't understand, yet
such unimaginable beauty.

THE QUIET CORE OF CHAOS

We live amid chaos whether we recognize
it or not. I choose to live on an island
away from the blare and glare of the city,

yet our island emerged from a violent birth,
rising from the depths of the sea, its craggy
face presenting a few miles distant from its

mainland mother. Volcanic eruptions
scattered agates along the shore,
a sudden disruptive upheaval.

The revelations of wind, the epiphany
of stars burning from the inside, blinking
their ancient stories into the shifting air.

Truth is always a bit odd. How meaning
may be found in the midst of chaos if
we listen, open ourselves to the risk

of what we might find inside. And isn't this
what art is all about?

THE LESSON OF PLUMS

After year-long illness, a dream.
My doctor stands in the center
of a cultivated field,
the furrows deep and straight.
His brown suit blends
with the richness of the dark soil.
Arms extended, palms open,
his words travel through
sunlit air: *You are ready to grow.*

So simple, so hackneyed,
yet when I awake I know it's over,
the illness that blew in
like a menacing wind and me
a trembling leaf clinging
to what I knew of strength—
now nearly floating
in an autonomy of lightness.

Sometimes it's not about
seeking but of receiving,
the way a plum takes in light,
an inner ripening that cracks
its perfect purple skin,
and sweetness, an amber rivulet,
crusts along the gash.

RED GIANTS AND WHITE DWARFS

For my part I know nothing with any certainty,
but the sight of the stars makes me dream.
~ Vincent van Gogh

For Emily

How can we know except by listening?
There is no certainty, no certainty at all,
except what hums to us through the mists
of our dreams, speaks through the voice of silence.

My granddaughter and I exchange quotes,
this quiet girl who travels beyond
her years, bonded by a longing
we cannot name.

We look to the stars, those burning
embers that fuel our yearnings,
that glitter in our imaginations:
red giants and white dwarfs.

Yes, how can we know except by listening?
They say stars are in constant conflict
with themselves: the gravity of collapsing inward,
the light that pushes back.

AND THEY DANCED BY THE
LIGHT OF THE MOON

Sly old moon, familiarity has not breached
your mysteries. You hold onto your secrets.
I am continually beguiled by the gleam
and shadow of your orbits.

A charismatic luminary, you pull us
toward you and we are helpless to resist.
Inner tides ebb and flow; the sea's
moods are faithful to your call.

You rise, cloaked in melancholy,
and I love that feeling, just on the edge
of sadness where I have no voice,
yet syllables arrange themselves
turning, tumbling into space
and I whisper, *Tell me, tell me.*

EBEY'S LANDING

Whidbey Island

I come to the shore when demands of everyday
grow heavy, float on waves of stillness,
calmed by rhythms of the sea.

The time between this and then—
a quiet moment when day fades into night,
or a clutch of seasons that span a lifetime.

I wait, standing on the edge
of the unknown—time salted with intensity,
serenity, hopefulness, uncertainty.

How to wait, yet capture the moment? How to
savor change, yet cling to the authenticity
of the fixed?

Is it longing for something beyond myself
that ripples deep within the mysterious
well of possibilities?

The poet says, *Don't try too hard. Just be.*
Slow down the words. See how light
informs the sea, how it plays counterpoint

to the tide, and mountains ghost to the horizon.

IMPLICATIONS OF GLASS

Answers to big questions rarely arrive
in one piece. Hints, even signs or signals,
rub against our intellect and we may,
or may not, catch the shine of their truth.

The bowl of sea glass on my library table
glistens in sunlight; broken shards tumbled
over stones for decades, now shaped
and transformed, speak of the past: a brown
spirits bottle, a cobalt blue liniment jar,
a green soda bottle, and turquoise bottles
that once held old-time elixirs.

Like tumbled glass, fragments of answers
may hide in everyday slices of life;
we just need time to put the pieces together.
Or, insight may be colored by lessons
from the past when we were buffeted
by tides of hardship and loss.

Yet, at times, a flash of knowing
comes suddenly. I think of this
as I hold a kaleidoscope to light,
one turn and tiny bits of glass fall
into place, fitting together perfectly.

THE WEIGHT OF WORDS

I'm trying to become more thoughtful
about spoken words; words that fly
into the air like broken-winged birds,

unlikely to soar on uplifted currents
of wisdom, perhaps to glide toward
a landscape of kindness and light.

Often, I choose silence,
an inner dialogue that considers
what I know of truth,

and I listen to what's said and not
said: sentences bent around the truth,
snapped in half and left hanging,

silence that can initiate a storm.
Bonhoeffer said, *Not to speak
is to speak*—those times

when words must carry the burden
of justice. So, what to set aside
and what to carry to the altar

of integrity? A daunting decision
knowing one may send blessings
or blight into the world.

I'm learning to be more cautious
before I speak, recalling that even eagles
exercise their wings before they fledge.

WHEN A MIRACLE SPEAKS

When a miracle speaks, don't be bashful.
Run right up to it. Hug it like an old friend.
Don't let go. Give it an extra squeeze.

Walk the beach with it. Talk about old times,
those moments when the vessel of love
overflowed. Listen to every word.

When a miracle speaks, there are no thunderous
lightning bolts. Hold the drama. It speaks
from the back row. Look around. It may be
closer than you think.

Sometimes a miracle whispers. Other times
the miracle eats ice cream at midnight,
wears argyle socks and a fedora,
dances until the sun is up.

Don't forget the hard times. The miracle was there;
it was just wearing old jeans and sunglasses
so as not to be blinded by your tears.

Why are you so shy of miracles? You're not the only
mystery. You have a common rhythm. It's in your DNA.
Sometimes I think you enjoy being dull.

It's as simple as this: When a miracle
speaks, answer.

CONFESSION

I am a syntaxer.
My sins are many.
I tax mostly myself.

I arrange symbols, hungering
for harmony; chase a relentless
notion that my marrow-language
matters.

Words pulse toward each other,
float into shuttered dreams,
tangled amid half-thoughts
and desires I sort through
searching for connections.

I struggle to honor inexpressible
feelings as I touch
a pussy willow bud, listen
to the hum of bees, notice
a sick man without stockings
hunched against a building.

Day and night, words skitter
over keys, tumbling locks
that link past with present.
I gather some in a vault
of safekeeping, hoard others
in recessed chambers,
exposing them one by one,
knowing they will
also expose me.

Taxed by words,
urged by words,
assuaged by words,
lexis bound: a syntaxer
showing no sign of remorse.

DAMP MAGIC

Consider the magical qualities of water.
Not the braided waterfalls that unfurl
down the mountain, the roar of the ocean,
nor the silvery slide of raindrops
cascading down the bedroom window.

Not even snowflakes, tiny frozen doilies
decorating the landscape, a white fairy tale
in a quiet world, or the gurgle
of a brook passing through a meadow.

Something curious happens in the shower,
while I'm rushing to get ready for a meeting;
bits and pieces of poems come gushing out,
infused in the hot water, and I fret
they will slip away, swirl down the drain,
before I can capture them.

Or while luxuriating in the bathtub,
words and images hook together,
float like clouds into the stream
of my consciousness, gauzy
irresistible lines of verse.

I'm sure I am not the only one
to experience the transforming power
of water, and what am I to do
when the creative urge wraps me
in its big soft terry-cloth towel
and leads me, dripping, to my desk?

GEOMETRY OF FAITH

In dreams I see rich tapestries shot
with golden thread: rose, green, and silver

arabesque patterns, galvanic charm
that glides out of sleep into the sunrise

of consciousness and rises like a dove,
not of this world—bliss, unexplained

except for the subconscious truth of beauty
and who am I to question?

Later, on public television, I chance
upon familiar kaleidoscopic images,

breath-taking magnificence: Mandelbrot's Set—
budding, branching, complex geometry

that masters chaos—sunflowers, leaves,
shells, zebras, snowflakes, cauliflower,

geckos, brains, arranged in like patterns,
self-similarity, internal consistency.

Some call it the thumbprint of God,
a design that links all and goes on forever.

THE WORLD BETWEEN

Loss needs no introduction.
Uninvited, it visits everyone.
Like a ruthless river
that overflows its banks,
it saturates all within its path,
changes course, creates
new channels, a new landscape
where nothing looks familiar.

Loss partners with change
the way wind alters the prospect
of clouds, transforming them
into new shapes, aligning
them with each other
in ever-changing compositions.

Loss questions what we knew
to be true, calls us to an unknown
perspective. How to find our way
suspended in a curious haze
of before and after? Perhaps we
must enter darkness to find light.

SYLLABLES OF WONDER

When I was a student nurse
working in the newborn nursery,
our family doctor, from my small hometown,
came to the city hospital to check on a baby
who needed his attention.

Too bad about your grandmother, he said.
What about my grandmother?
Oh, I thought you knew. She had a stroke.

My dear grandmother who taught me
the language of the countryside. We picked
blackberries, gathered mushrooms, cut
and dried cascara bark.

I kneeled amid bleeding hearts and trillium
that grew rampant in the forest, a small child
learning to pray.

She taught the syllables of wonder
while Northern Lights spread watercolor
glory across the sky;

and the delights of everyday
when we stood in the cold clear creek
as it washed summer dust from our feet.

Is it kind to withhold what might be hurtful?
Although my family thought to spare me,
they soon realized nothing could keep me
from her side.

KINTSUGI

Brokenness is not always obvious.
We don't hear the crack or splatter.

We wear an amulet of denial to protect
ourselves from the perceptions of others.

Is it possible we have been vulnerable
from the beginning, living within fragile shells?

A sudden blow, a series of subtle traumas,
may shatter our protection.

Unlike an egg dropped on a tile floor,
we have to believe we can be restored.

Perhaps we are not what we once were,
but we are not damaged.

Think of the Japanese who repair a broken vase
with gold, highlighting its flaws to add beauty

and, in so doing, the repaired vessel becomes
stronger.

A GLORIOUS WEBBING

It should be about the fragrance, but it's not.
It's about the sweet pea lashing itself
to the wire fence so tightly
tendrils must be cut to free the flower
and I'm drawn to the notion and need of bonds—

how a mother's arms and breast and voice
enclose the babe in a tender cocoon
of connection; how we link lives as we begin
an uncertain passage through crossroads of choice.

Friends have touched me with healing hands,
provided a cup of grace, pointed the way,
and waved me through. Do we really appreciate
how much we need each other?

C.S. Lewis said, *We read to know
we are not alone.* We need the comfort
of words to connect us to stories, intensely
personal, satisfyingly communal.

We need the shared celebration of art:
creativity that resides in all of us and feels
like a prayer to happiness.

We are troubadours who need each other's
music—to soar on currents of another's
inspiration, catch beauty that floats
through air, enters the body, spirals down
into the depths of who we are.

I once witnessed newborn twins, moments old,
resting on their mother's chest.

One twin touches the hand of the other,
and that twin grasps the hand that is offered—
holds on.

OPTICAL ILLUSION

The eye receives color, shape,
and light, but the eye does not
recognize certain shades of gray—
the dimming of certainties,
pale fluttering questions,
shifting kaleidoscopic choices.

The eye cannot identify
the hard shape of loss,
the void of loneliness,
or a tight circle of friends.

The eye admits light, but holds it
for its own purposes. It cannot
perceive how sunlight pierces
the prisms of raindrops causing
colors to explode, or that I see sunlight
flicker through eucalyptus leaves
when my lids are closed. It cannot
know what the heart squeezes
out of every beat—the red blood
of wonder.

THE QUESTION OF HAPPINESS

Does happiness carry danger
in its heart?

A dagger waiting to plunge into
the chest of joy.

An affliction we suffer in the midst
of unbroken contentment.

Perhaps we turn from those quiet moments
that need no explanation, elevated moments

that rush toward bliss, as if too much
happiness portends misfortune.

Love rises to the edge of risk,
balances on the possibility of loss—

a journey down an uncertain road,
no promises along the way.

Don't we owe it to ourselves and others
to pursue happiness?

Walking into the sun, I can't see
what's ahead, can't see into the shadows

until I'm in them.

SPRING SOLSTICE

March 20, 2019

Middle of the night and sleep
a distant horizon. Brightness

of the super moon electrifies
the darkness, an ethereal glow

that defies the hour, and my mind
travels long-forgotten roads,

mostly rural, some bumpy and pot-holed,
to a small town where we grew up

wide-eyed and trusting. We have stayed
in touch, my high school classmates,

dear friends who gather each year by the river
for a reunion. We are old now.

One man, just diagnosed with lung cancer,
says, *It makes me feel better just to see all of you,*

and it may be that we see each other as we were:
bobby socks, poodle skirts, hot rods, ducktail hair.

I marvel at how perception defies the years.

SHELTERING IN PLACE

April, 2020

I want to remember this time,
this time of waiting. We are like
spring bulbs emerging little by little
through the dark earth, holding
future promise tightly within ourselves.

I want to remember the gradual dawning
of danger, how it feels to be removed
from what we knew to be true.

They say suffering involves loss of control.
It is thrust upon us and although I've
settled into this different way of being,
the ache is bone-deep for those taken
beyond a quiet island of isolation.

I want to remember our pressing need
for each other. This yearning to touch,
skin to skin, to authenticate what is
fine and just and joyful.

Now the apple tree is setting blossoms.
A dove is cooing from across the field.
As I rise from my labors in the garden
the calming scent of lavender clings
to my clothes.

DRAGONFLY

As a group they're called a dazzle.
They open windows of imagination,

and the flashing iridescence of sunlight
on fragile wings, the delicate symmetry,

lifts us toward this metaphor in flight.
Blinded by the glare of beauty, a ballet

of grace and elegance, we fail to see
the strong mandible, the sharp edges

of strength that can crush prey
in one bite.

SETTING THINGS RIGHT

It feels good to set things right
and when we can't, to do
what we can in another way.

The rhythm of knitting needles
lining up stitches in perfect order.
Numbers in the ledger agreeing
at the end of the month.
The smooth vibrations of the old
Massey Ferguson after adjustments
have been made.

This morning, weeding in my herb garden,
I inhale rosemary's essence, conjure images
of the bubbling sauce. Close by, tarragon
for creamy mushroom pasta,
lavender, lovage, and thyme.

A hummingbird comes jazzing by,
its flight an improvisation of zip and dazzle.
This little rufous knows where he's been
and where he's going.

It feels good to set things right
and for a time, here and now,
I can make things better. The world
feels less tilted and sunlight illuminates
the edges of everything.

CIRCLE OF TWO

We need to belong, the way crows ink
their signatures on a tablet of sky

and autumn leaves titter in the wind,
a dance of take and release.

This pairing, a natural ripening
like the fullness of wheat in midday sun.

Even the extroverted moon, so far distant,
calls and we answer with longing

that seals our lips with thwarted
words. Now rosehips and snowberries

riot in roadside thickets,
a complement of winter contrast,

and in the mountains, bighorn sheep
follow ancient paths to arrive

where they belong.

PARABLE OF A CARB LOVER

Lola is irresistible in spite of her issues,
which are many.

The eyes of this yellow lab plead,
Love me, just love me.

She arrived at my niece Lauren's house unannounced,
a note tucked into her collar which read, *Lola.*

The mischief began straightaway when she ate lipstick
from Lauren's purse, then consumed half

of a Papa Murphy's pizza. Her noshing misdeeds
have included an entire loaf of artisan jalapeno bread,

a beautifully decorated gingerbread cake,
six double chocolate fudge protein bars,

a blackberry pie left cooling on the counter,
the plate licked clean, having never left the countertop.

A loaf of bread stolen from a neighbor's garage,
cuticle oils, hand lotion, anything that smells slightly sweet,

candy left out during the holidays, anything edible
under or on the Christmas tree.

Lauren believes Lola is *a gift from God. She is so imperfect*
she teaches me over and over, no matter how imperfect

and flawed I am, I am loved.

MIDDLE OF THE NIGHT MUSINGS

You don't need a reason to be happy.
I don't know who said that—oh,
I think it was me.

I'm not obliged to notice how
cherry cream scones on the tea tray
wave Scottish flags.

How my sweetie and I share a compass
directed toward an unmistakable magnet,
its needle steady and true.

How the newborn curls on my chest
in sleep, swaddled in a blanket
of trust.

How snow comes in the night,
hushes the island, cozies us
around the hearth's crackling flames.

How a hummingbird appears, a flash
of jazz in the midst of winter's
soliloquy.

How the deer come every morning
to my window, plead with luminous
eyes for me to bring them apples.

Or how raindrops bead on the window,
gather and run together, a cascade
of opalescent harmony.

How sunrise burns its greeting into the day
and sunset's disappearing radiance
signals rest.

I believe you don't need a reason
to be happy, but having reasons
is a delicious start.

GENDER BIAS

No girls allowed, but
we didn't care—those
grimy boys, grubbing
in the dust of the playground.

Recess bell and they scrambled
to the same spot, scribing
a circle in the dirt and tossing
in their marbles.

We heard the names: Aggies,
Cat's Eyes, Benningtons,
Bonker, Popper, Bumboozer,
Biggie. The Steelie, a shiny
ball bearing, a gift of grace
from a father's repair project,
seemed high and mighty
among the fragile glass spheres.

The boys crowded around the circle,
pulling shooters out of their pockets
and each had a favorite flicking technique:
first finger, middle finger, or thumb.
A strong shot was needed to knock
a marble out of the ring.

We girls, who danced and sang inside
the rhymical ropes of Double Dutch,
were definitely outside the ring
and glad of it.

EBEY'S PRAIRIE

We live on a prairie in the middle of an island.
Our prairie, a small tray of land bordered
by a cemetery that cradles the pioneers,
ends at a bluff that drops to the sea.

Where indigenous people once harvested camas,
native grasses are all but gone, tamed into fields
of wheat and barley and oats.

Island wind blows over the prairie.
The crops and grasses that remain
rise to its will in green and gold waves
that rush to meet those rolling in from the sea.

Rich prairie soil yields to the plow, allows
for growth. Like the seeds that sprout
there, we have a chance to ripen and grow,
open to a larger force that shapes us,
moving us to something beyond ourselves.

THE ELEGANCE OF AGEING

Old Barn, Watercolor
~ Keith Fakkema

The old barn stands alone, its weathered boards
a testament to the hot breath of summers past,
the pounding fists of winter storms.

Early morning, I hear a rooster crow and milk pails
clanking, see the dance of dust motes in the loft,
remember the pungent smell of fresh manure,
grain in burlap sacks, the warmth of cows
fitting their heads through stanchions
at milking time.

Now the barn, once sheltering,
is open to sky. What do the empty
spaces say? Silence lingers like rests
between notes of a cherished song.

Some would claim this relic from another
time has slipped beyond its usefulness, yet
it stands open to air and light. Swallows
fly in and out and find a home.

WHY HAVE FAVORITES?

A house on a hill. A leather-bound book.

Lilies of the valley. Swans.

New-mown hay. Cezanne's art.

The porch on a summer day. White peaches.

The Secret Garden. A child's laughter.

Walking in fog. Lavender.

Amadeus, the movie. Fresh Dungeness crab.

Louie singing *It's a Wonderful World.*

Snowflakes. Rum raisin ice cream.

That blue-green color deep in the swirls
of Deception Pass.

Sunlight through stained glass windows.

Oscar Peterson's *Hymn to Freedom.*

If you don't have favorites, how do you
make each day special?

THE LONESOME TIME

Sunday afternoons, when we were kids,
our father took us for rides on country backroads.
We twisted around mountains, followed
the curve and chuckle of rivers, passed through
cool shadows in deep canyons, and skirted the coast.

Whenever we drove across Deception Pass Bridge
onto Whidbey Island, at a certain place, in an open field,
on a bluff overlooking Admiralty Inlet, my father
would say, *I'd like to build a house right here someday.*

He died when he was fifty-seven, too soon
for that dream to settle into reality. Now,
years later, I live just down the road
from that open field, on a bluff overlooking
Admiralty Inlet. His grandchildren
and great-grandchildren come to visit.
They love the island as he did, as I do.

I scan the inlet for incoming vessels
as evening light delegates passage
to memories. It is the lonesome time,
just before darkness sets in.

THE SCENT OF MEMORIES

The freshness of summer drifts through
my bedroom window and, for a moment,
I'm suspended in time, as if I'd forgotten
the scent of grass, the fragrant
exhalations of earth.

I remember my young self
almost hidden in tall grass, fingering
bleeding hearts that grew wild
and somehow touched the wild
yearnings of my naive heart.

Lying in the backyard on the cushiony lawn,
a dreamy canopy of clouds overhead,
I transformed them into whatever
I wanted them, and me, to be.

How is it we let go of the simple things
that ground us—forget the smell of dark soil,
of mosses, leaves, and clover?

I wander with the child, the young girl,
the woman, a wife, a mother; my life
a vine, twining around seasons
of loss and joy.

Now the sweet silence of twilight,
the purple glow of approaching darkness
a gentle comfort.

From

ALMANAC OF QUIET DAYS
2021

Ekphrastic Poetry
Emily Gibson Photography

NATURE'S HUSH

Something has quieted the poet's voice.
Something on the edge of mystery.

Is dawn rising in the mists of morning?
Has the first frost of autumn cooled the air?

Maples gleam in harmony with the season;
how easily they release what is no longer needed.

In the bounty of pasture, two Haflingers graze
the contented comfort of togetherness.

How to settle into serenity such as this?
Ask the silence. Ask the light.

RIPENING SEASON

Seed heads will start to nod or bow on the stem
when they are ready to harvest.

Ancient grains, that nourish and sustain, show
us when they are ripe. Oh, that we could come
to our own maturity with such assurance.

False starts, wrong turns, trials, pain, pinches
of regret. Lessons of patience and humility.

I think of this as we travel through the Palouse,
the fine golden shine of wheat and barley fields
spread in undulating slopes and knolls to the horizon.

Under the persistent urging of sunlight,
the grain grows and ripens, giving itself
to harvest and to the eventual warmth
of a baker's hands. Then, kneading,
stretching, lightness, and rising.

ROAD TRIP

The poem travels, and no one knows
where it's going. It tours scenic
byways, roaming in and around hills
and valleys, searching for pockets of truth.

Soon enough the poem encounters a blind
corner, a steep upgrade, a sheer drop-off.
It trembles and is jolted by unexpected
bumps and potholes.

Like a young person, the poem must journey
alone: a time of separation to test and explore,
and eventually return to where it began.

With time, it travels the backroads of memory,
an arduous passage, rich with promise
and risk.

Along the way, it basks in the early morning
gleam of a wheat field, the silver shine of the sea,
and in the silence of a forest it finds rest.
As sunlight pours down the trunks of ancient
evergreens, the poem follows the light
and finds its way.

AN INVITATION

Each day comes wrapped in choices
tied with the twine of possibilities.
Tug a frayed edge, your life
tumbles out.

Think of the farmer who trusts
the promise of soil to grow
the wheat; his vision of sturdy
hands that will knead the dough,
shape the loaves, and of the patience
to wait for rising.

Come break a morsel from the loaf.
Dip into the lemon curd and honey.

HARVEST BEE

After college, and a few years away,
he came back to the family farm.
For many years he lived the seasons,
accommodating the weather, reconciling
himself to the land.

There in the Palouse, he tended undulating
fields of wheat, twelve hundred acres
planted and harvested each year.

Winter saw the fields seeded, green shoots
of spring pushing through the soil,
and by summer, wheat nodding and bowing
in honor of its ripeness.

When they heard, they came. Neighbors,
nearby and those fifty miles away,
climbed into combines and grain trucks,
as word spread over the Palouse
that cancer had disabled one of their own.

He watched as sixty farmers orchestrated
the harvest: a composition of precise movements,
a triumph of goodness, bringing in the crop
in six hours, work that would have taken him
three weeks to complete.

CATHEDRAL OF LIGHT

See how sunlight falls
into a forest creating columns
of shadow and slanted brightness?

Light slides down the trunks of silent
evergreens, partners with the wind
to excite quaking aspens.

It does not give itself to everything,
barely touching the cool damp pockets
where moss fronds glisten,

and crumbled remains of fallen
cedars molder in a hollow
of aromatic scent.

The forest awakens and the light
unraveling in darkness sends
rays as pure as love.

THE ENCHANTED FOREST

The children found an opening
in the woods and named it
The Enchanted Forest.

Grandpa bent willow branches
to make miniature chairs and table.
A teapot, tiny cups, and flowers.

Imaginations soared beyond
the overhanging trees, and when
Grandma slipped a jar of jellybeans

into the dense cool darkness
of the camp, the children were afraid
to partake, certain the candy

had been put there by a conniving witch.

FENCES

Why is it we may see barbs
as we contemplate a new adventure?

Are we afraid of a little pain?
Is what we want worth
a few scratches?

We are on the outside looking in.
If all we see are obstacles, isn't that a way
of wounding ourselves?

This late summer morning, fog softens
the golden seed pods of wild carrots,
and fern fronds bend inward.

See beyond, that green valley rimmed
with evergreens? Step inside your dreams.
Think about what may be there
waiting to get out.

A fence offers protection, but is also
a choice between confinement
or freedom.

BOOKWORM

You know who you are.

You are the person who stockpiles stacks of books
on the bedside table and next to your favorite chair.

The person who sacrifices sleep to read
just one more page.

The person who reads the cereal box when
nothing else is available near the breakfast table.

The girl who falls into an uncovered manhole
walking down a busy street while reading.

The objects of your affection may be
as precious as the *Book of Kells*

or as sappy as an Archie and Jughead
comic book.

It's the words, the words,
that keep zipping by, telegraphing

an urgent message: *What's next?*
What's next?

FRAGILE BEAUTY

It's just a leaf. A damaged leaf at that,
clinging to a filbert tree ravaged by blight.
The leaf turns partially back upon itself,
riddled with holes, the traumatic result
of voracious insect appetites.

Damaged does not accurately describe
this leaf, the color of rich burgundy wine,
deep purple veins that branch to the tips
of its serrated edge. The holes open the leaf
to light and air, forming a filigree of nature,
an exquisite fragile beauty.

It makes me think of our own traumas,
how they open us, raw and hurting, humble us,
soften and expand us to the pain of others,
and when we are most vulnerable, we hold on,
weakened, but not necessarily damaged.
Perhaps it is then our scars become beautiful
and an inner loveliness shines through.

TREE HOUSE

Everyone needs a place of their own.
A place to nurture dreams, evaluate

secrets. Climb upward, pull
the rope ladder up behind you.

Settle into the sturdy arms
of the black walnut tree.

Listen.
Enter the silence.

Let your thoughts fly
without destination.

The breeze soothes like a gentle
spirit. Rest and find

the matchless part of yourself.

MOUNT SHUKSAN

I go to the mountains where sky
paints the foothills blue,
where cedar, hemlock, and noble fir
lend their hues to the river, and sweet air
carries the resinous scent of evergreens
to itself.

Sunlight seeps into the deep darkness
of forest, spilling across the trunks
of the massive trees, brightening
the berries of salal and Oregon grape.

Above the lake, Mount Shuksan
raises its stony, snow-clad face
to all that is possible and I am
diminished and expanded
by its presence.

SNOW GEESE

I wish I could show you how a blizzard

    of snow geese rose from furrowed

white-flocked fields, at this very spot,

    and billowed around the steeple

of the Conway Lutheran Church.

They ascended wind currents, swirling

    like satin ribbons, light as bridal veils.

Their black-tipped wings played chromatic

    scales in octaves of sky as they rose higher

      in the silver light of winter,

        an aria soaring beyond

          our earthbound awe.

COUNSEL TO A TEENAGER

An adorable granddaughter
in a family of boys.
We bought her a silver bracelet,
year after year adding a charm
to mark events in her life.

Baby slippers, a heart,
a lighthouse, ferry boat,
and sand dollar; a book,
a flute, a ballerina,
the Eiffel Tower.

For her fifteenth birthday
Grandpa picked out a little frog.
Very cute, but of what significance?

When he gave it to her he said,
*This is a reminder: Don't be kissing
any toads. They never turn into
charming princes.*

A CURIOUS KNOWING

Before markers appear,
there is a time when you pause,
as if you hear a call. Something
has shifted. Is it the air?
A scent? A curious knowing
that comes without facts.
Summer has turned toward fall.

Later autumn will show itself
with undisguised confidence,
wild color, crisp morning light,
and the wind will page through
a catalog of leaves.

INNOVATION

An ancient object that began
as ornamental: bronze, sterling,
and gold buttons displayed
on the clothing of those
who enjoyed prosperity
and privilege.

Ages and ages before someone
thought to design a hole
into which a button would fit.
Amazing how long
it sometimes takes, for us
to figure out how to bring
things together.

PITCHFORK GRACE

If these boots could talk they'd say,
Let's get it done.

Striding to the barn before dawn,
mud squishing under the soles,
stalls cleaned, horses fed.

Along the wood-chipped path
to the chopping block where axe
divides lengths of alder into firewood.

Up the rise that leads to the pasture,
fences in need of mending, and beyond
to fields of hay lying in windrows
waiting to be baled.

One careful foot after the other
in the cultivated garden, potatoes
unearthed, and on to the orchard,
up rungs of a ladder, golden apples
nestled into baskets.

At day's end, pulled off and left
in a bright kitchen on a braided rug
just inside the door.
Muck, mud, and manure the reward
for a good day of honest work.

POETS AND RODENTS

Fluffle

What poet could resist the word?
We gather words as if dictionaries
would soon be banned, tuck them
into the recesses of our minds,
horde them in overflowing journals.

We chew on words enjoying the crunch,
the taste, the subtle flavors, an addiction
not responsive to therapy or rehab sessions.

We are like a *gathering of wild rabbits,*
adorable creatures that were once considered
rodents: gnawing mammals with an extra set
of large incisors.

ONE ROOM

An old abandoned schoolhouse,
the only relief as the prairie stretches
in unrelenting flatness to the horizon.

From where did the children come?
Where did they go? I can hear
their giggles. I hear them singing.

I can see their drawings of teepees
and buffalo on the walls, see
girls dressed in gingham frocks,
and suspenders hung from the thin
shoulders of boys.

I smell paste, and the biscuits and ham
in their lunch pails. Hear the school bell?
See them clambering out the door
into the wind? Into the world?

Old buildings speak with alluring voices,
holding deep mysteries inside.

The old schoolhouse is about to fall
but it tilts forward as if it feels
the thrust of lives that have moved
through that classroom and the hope
that abides in learning.

PEACEFUL VALLEY

I admire how my cousin answers the call
of restless seas, sailing to exotic places,
freedom of wind and salt air riddled
with danger; outwitting storms
and pirates who clamber aboard.

I favor a quiet life: a sunlit garden,
tranquil pools of reflection, the mercy
of days that blend into a peaceful whole.

The two of us were driving to Mt. Baker,
winding up a narrow road, when we saw it.
The road was narrow, we couldn't stop,
so we turned around and went back,
and it was as if disorder had been relegated
to a distant realm.

Here a valley tucked into the foothills
of the Cascade Range, the air spiked
with the fragrance of evergreens
and mown fields. Autumn color
gentle in its arrival.

I could sink into the stillness
of this countryside. Yet I think of those
who thrive on the thrill of danger
and uncertainty—consider how
to balance the kindness of peace
with the abundance of adventure.

Coda

AMETHYST

From the window above my writing table
morning light, dulled by low hanging clouds,
tints the bay amethyst. Rose thickets pick up
winter's palette, a muted burgundy in a field
of green.

The book is finished, poems tucked
between covers that signal something
more: a repository of longings,
the unveiling of an inner life.
Now a quiet emptiness descends,
not depletion, more an awareness
of waiting, not knowing what will come
next, or if there is the necessity of a next.

The day stretches out its arms, a courier
to all that is possible, right here, right now.
A blade of grass bent to allow the lingering
slide of dew, denuded willows that permit
us to see through, and at the harbor
an empty ferry slip—travelers waiting
for passage to the other side.

ACKNOWLEDGMENTS

Grateful acknowledgments to the editors of the following publications in which these poems first appeared.

"American Gothic": *Soundings Review*

"Biopsy": *Connecticut River Review*

"Café Terrace at Night": *Birmingham Art Journal*

"Cascade Suite": *Mobius Magazine*

"Choices We Make When We are Too Young to Make Them": *Poet's Touchstone*

"Cookie Bakers": *Literary Mama*

"Ebey's Landing": *Mizmor Anthology*

"East of the Mountains": *Adanna: Women and War, a Tribute to Adrienne Rich*

"Green Apple on Black Plate": *Cascade; Birmingham Arts Journal*

"Hobo Pride": *Insights: A Notebook, Cyberwit*

"House of Guesses": *Soundings Review*

"Luncheon on the Grass": *Adanna: A Journal for Women*

"Old Church Pew": *Soundings Review*

"Private Man": *Borderlands: Texas Poetry Review*

"Small Town Coffee Shop": (World Enough Writer's Anthology) *Coffee Poems*

"Smiting Dragons": *Phrasings*

"Song for the Road": (Tall Grass Writer's Guild) *Black and White Anthology*

"Sourdough": *Sandy River Review*

"The Lesson of Plums": *Adanna: Women and War, A Tribute to Adrienne Rich*

"The Theory of Everything": *Poems in the Waiting Room*

"Tilt": *The Westmorland Award, Westmorland Arts and Heritage Festival*

"Wellington Train Disaster": (Midwest Writing Center) *Off Channel Anthology*

"What Brings Us to Water": (Washington Poet's Association Anthology) *Tattoos on Cedar; Floating Bridge Review*

"When All Has Been Said": *Quill and Parchment*

"Where Poems Winter": *Upper Delaware Writer's Collective*

"Wolf Moon": (Outrider Press Anthology) *The Moon*

"Yellowstone Park, 1948": (Write Wing Publishing) *Through a Distant Lens*

"Yesterday's Light": (Write Wing Publishing) *Through a Distant Lens*

And grateful acknowledgments to editors of the presses that published the seven collections in which many of the poems in this collection previously appeared:

What Brings Us to Water, Poetica Publishing Award, 2010

What's to be Done with Beauty, Creative Justice Press Award, 2012

Night Beyond Black, MoonPath Press, 2016

Glint, MoonPath Press, 2019

Road Signs and Hobo Marks, Cyberwit, 2020

The Lesson of Plums, MoonPath Press, 2020

Almanac of Quiet Days, Cyberwit, 2021

My thanks to editor, Lana Ayers, for her perceptive guidance and generous spirit. Heartfelt praise to Tonya Namura for her beautiful design work. It is a pleasure to work with both of these talented women. I am grateful!

Thanks to Sheryl Clough, Diane Stone, and Teresa Wiley who provide insightful and helpful comments as we share our love of poetry, and to Lorraine Healy who was with me at the beginning.

Special thanks to my longtime friend, Lillian Toop, who is always there for me with an open heart, quick wit, and laughter.

Deepest thanks and gratitude to my family whose creativity and abundant love inspire me every day.

ABOUT THE AUTHOR

Lois Parker Edstrom, a retired nurse, is the author of two chapbooks and six full length collections of poetry. She has received two Hackney National Literary Awards, the Outrider Press Grand Prize, the Westmoreland Award, and the Benefactor's Award from Whidbey Island Writer's Association. Her poems have appeared in numerous literary journals and anthologies, been read by Garrison Keillor on *The Writer's Almanac*, and featured in Ted Kooser's *American Life in Poetry*.

Edstrom's career in nursing and her poetic passion coalesced when her poetry appeared in *Poems in the Waiting Room*, a publication furnished to hospitals and doctors' offices in New Zealand. Her poetry has been translated into Braille, and adapted to dance by the Bellingham Repertory Dance Company. The natural beauty of Whidbey Island, where she lives with her husband, inspires much of her work.

www.ingramcontent.com/pod-product-compliance
Ingram Content Group UK Ltd.
Pitfield, Milton Keynes, MK11 3LW, UK
UKHW040620170225
4623UKWH00017B/134